MISSIONARY POSITION

A slightly irreverent guide to sex after purity culture

CELESTE HOLBROOK, PHD

For more information, email info@drcelesteholbrook.com.

ISBN: 978-1-968164-93-5 (Paperback)

ISBN: 978-1-968164-95-9 (eBook)

This is dedicated to my daughters, Ella and Zoe, and to my incredible clients.

May you find pleasure without shame.

Foreword

by Jen Hatmaker

I got married at nineteen. I can't help you process that insanity, so just do your best. I grew up in a precious, Southern Baptist environment without much input from the normal(?) world. To this day, my friends play a game where they ask me what I think an Urban Dictionary sexual term means, and I proceed to get it entirely wrong while they lie on the floor laughing. (I display similar remediation around drinking terms, like calling a morning drink after a bender "the tail of the dog.")

I received exactly one sex talk from a parent. In an unfortunate turn of events, it was with my dad in fifth grade. A man of many words, we were deep in the bag on terms, parts, mechanics; I blacked out when he used the phrase "pleasurable for both parties." Mom put a book on my nightstand about periods, and you have now reached the end of my sexual education.

Well, not exactly. I was highly trained in purity culture, which squeamish Baptist parents outsourced to the local youth pastors. We signed up for True Love Waits™ at our churches and went through eight weeks of abstinence programming. The curriculum was void of any genuine sexual instruction, but it was rife with shame. It was traumatizing and set an entire generation up for sexual dysfunction.

During the opening session, my particular youth pastor held up a gorgeous red rose in full bloom and said: "Isn't this flower beautiful, everyone?" We all agreed that it was. We were slaying our coursework so far. He went on: "Girls" (the boys were strangely omitted from this demonstration), "right now you are like this lovely rose. The most beautiful, perfect gift. But when you start giving your body to your little boyfriends, you destroy the gift."

At this terrifying statement, he started plucking the petals off the rose:

"You let him touch your body." Pluck.

"You take off your clothes." Pluck.

"You engage in inappropriate acts." Pluck.

"You have sexual intercourse." Pluck.

"Until all you have to offer your husband on your wedding night is this . . . " At this point, the pastor held up the empty stick plucked of its petals, a pauper's gift if I ever saw one. Apparently there was no coming back from being a slutty, stripped rose. Who would ever want to marry a ruined stick?

We assimilated seven more weeks of curriculum, which focused on lassoing our impure thoughts in service to God. What are we looking at, what are we wearing, what are we listening to, what are we thinking about, *just how depraved were we?* No one taught us about actual, incredible sex. No one explained that sexual curiosity was normal and appropriate. It was cast as undisciplined, immoral, filthy, and un-Christian. Not only were we dirty, we were absolutely ruining our future marriages. That is, if we could find anyone who wanted to marry a barren stick.

So, it is no surprise I had to work endlessly to overcome this early programming. I took such shame and fear into my young marriage. I had to leave that purity environment entirely to even find vibrant conversations about sex; don't get me started on how long it took to prioritize female pleasure. Experimentation, toys, adventure, becoming the expert on my own body—these were the joys of adulthood I discovered long after I walked an aisle.

Because I lead so many women, I know with certainty this culture plagued millions of us. And it is not unique to the Baptists obviously; most religious cultures snuffed out healthy sexual development. Add body shaming, gender expectations, and the relentless patriarchy, and it is a wonder any of us managed to have vibrant sex lives.

But there is good news. This internal messaging can be unlearned. It is literally never too late. Sex can become exciting and fun, fulfilling and sensual. We have permission to rewrite the story. We can experience a sexual renaissance no matter our age, our relational status, or our history. Of all the categories to throw in the towel, *this is not the one.* Get excited, reader, because your life is about to change.

The book you are holding is a portal into a sex life you didn't even know existed. Celeste is hilarious and safe, unselfconscious and practical. You're about to receive tools, scripts, instruction, and pep talks should you need them. I've put her in front of my enormous community so many times because I haven't found her equal in this conversation. (She once showed up to my house to film an e-course on good sex with a bag of travel-sized vibrators for the whole crew.)

We need a guide we can trust. One who cares about our complicated histories while also gently pushing us toward exciting new frontiers. We need a leader who tends our damaged sexual souls who also tells us which vibrator to try. This is Celeste. She is the expert we've always wanted, and I am telling you this: you are on your way to the sex life of your dreams.

If your history involves a single sex talk in fifth grade with your dad, or a tutorial that compares your body to a dead rose, or any other number of horrors, you are in the right place. It is about to be a whole new day. I'm so excited for you.

With great love,

Jen Hatmaker

Table of Contents

Introduction

I don't feel like having sex. Ever.

I wish I wanted sex more.

I'm not really attracted to my partner.

I fantasize about other people.

I've never had an orgasm.

My partner wants to do things I don't want to do.

I don't feel like my body is sexy.

I masturbate. Is that okay?

I can't look at or touch my genitals. Is that okay?

I feel like sex is not for me, and I just want to do it for him.

I'm concerned I don't look (or taste) good to my partner.

I have faked all my orgasms.

I want more sex than my partner does.

I don't get aroused for sex.

Sex is painful.

Am I normal?

Have you ever had any of these thoughts? I certainly have had many of them, and so have many of my clients. The common denominator and root of all of these statements is harmful, neglectful purity culture messaging. Of course, other factors exist. But a colossal part of why so many women have these thoughts is that we were taught to think about sex through a religious lens not built for women.

As a sex educator, I spend most of my time speaking to people about their sex lives. My first priority with a new client is to help her feel safe. To help her feel known, seen, and validated. In that moment, she is the most important person in my life. She is telling me experiences and feelings she's never told anybody, and I take that seriously.

Feeling known and seen when talking about your sex life is a priority because sex makes us feel so vulnerable. You need a *trusted* person or partner who can hold that vulnerability for you in a very contained and gentle way.

So, I'd like to introduce myself and begin garnering your trust.

My name is Celeste, and I love hermit crabs, romantasy (Cassian forever), trail running, theater, sex education advocacy . . . and did I mention I love to read smut? I have identical twin daughters who were born in 2012 and a very kind husband with a fine-ass beard and an eye for interior design. I love my dogs, I think horses are magical creatures, and I've been a vegetarian since birth.

I am also Celeste—a woman who enjoys sex.

Do you notice any weirdness coming up in your chest when you read that last bit? This is because we aren't encouraged to talk about sex.

Salt-N-Pepa wildly took on the social norms of never talking about sex when they talked about sex in plain language in one of their hit songs, "Let's Talk About Sex." Of course, their music video was scrutinized for being far too sexual. This is exactly why they created the song. It was a response to the policing of women's sexuality and the way we avoided plain-language conversations about sex.

Here we are decades later, and talking about sex remains difficult. We *see* a lot more sex, from Netflix to porn and car commercials to cartoons. We have even sexualized fruit emojis. Sex is everywhere. But even in the face of an oversexualized culture, talking about sex in real, practical, plain-language ways is weirdly tough. Even if you were fortunate enough to have been raised by a set of caregivers who were unafraid to talk about sex in plain language, sexual communication remains elusive.

Why is this?

Do we feel that we will be judged if we talk about sex? Were we told it was bad, wrong, or sinful to have sex, much less think or talk about it? Do we feel that people will think differently of us?

Do we feel that we will think differently of ourselves? Are we scared that if we talk about sex, we are destined to be labeled as explicit? If we talk about sex, are we narcissistic? Too confident? Oversexualized? Gross?

If we talk about sex, are we . . . *dirty*?

So we don't talk about it. We don't say anything. Or, at least, we say very little.

If we do dare talk about sex, it is usually in times of crisis or dismay. Very few of us talk about our *good* sex.

I understand that reading a book about sex and purity culture while asking yourself questions about your own sex life could be weird, uncomfortable, or, at the very least, awkward.

I want you to know your feelings about sex are valid. Your thoughts, emotions, and experiences about sex are sacred, even if they are not normative or are possibly skewed, negative, or contradictory.

I see you, and I hold your thoughts and experience with reverence.

You're not silly for wanting more out of your sex life.

You are not broken for never wanting sex.

You are not weird for wanting something outside of what you think is a sexual "norm."

You are not flawed because sex is difficult.

You are not too much if you want more sex.

You are perfect and enough already, in this moment.

I'm here for you. To the best of my ability, I am going to help you see yourself. I'm here to make the process of healing from purity culture and addressing your sex life as comfortable as possible. This is my work, and I'm confident in it because I've done the work myself. I've weathered the storm. I've dug out of the snow. I'm reaching back to get you out too.

This book is about taking the *missionary position* of self-reclamation. You are going to save yourself from the harmful ideology of purity culture. By the time you reach the end of this book, I want you to feel lighter and more informed. I want you to be equipped to lovingly release yourself from the sexual messages you were given growing up and free to embrace the definitions and behaviors of sexual pleasure that are uniquely yours.

I'm nothing if not practical, so this book is set up to be a combination of theory and practice: praxis. I want you to not only uncover your own sexual story but also to know what to do in your sex life to rewire yourself for a new story.

I have divided the manuscript into four sections, each representing a step in the process of healing your sex life from the effects of purity culture. Each step is guided by your inner missionary. According to our new definition, "missionaries" are the women within us who embark on a sacred journey to rescue us from the confines of purity culture. They are not sent to save others but rather to liberate us from the shame, repression, and weight of expectations that were never ours to carry.

Meet your inner missionary team:

The Analyst: The mind, the strategist. She **names the problem,** maps out the terrain, and identifies the internalized scripts about sex holding her back. Her work is essential because you can't dismantle what you don't see, and you can't go forward without having a guiding purpose.

The Assassin: The fire, the disruptor. She **obliterates shame,** cuts through the lies, and honestly addresses toxic messaging by safeguarding and honoring your younger self. This is where the rage and protection live.

The Healer: The heart, the nurturer. After the old beliefs are slashed, she steps in **to soothe the wounds** left behind. She reteaches what was never taught, offering new narratives of pleasure, worth, and sex.

The Explorer: The body, the adventurer. With a new foundation in place, she **steps into desire, play, and curiosity,** engaging with sexuality on her own terms and free from past constraints. She embraces novelty and walks boldly into new sexual beginnings.

I hope that by the end of this book, you will have unhooked and rewritten your sexual story and have acquired the tools you need to create lasting pleasure and clarity in your sex life. I want you to feel liberated, free, flourishing, and strong.

I hope you learn to own pleasure and *save yourself.*

Author's Note: Is This a Religious Book?

"If God exists, I'm pretty sure They don't give a crap about my vibrators." —Me

No, this isn't a religious book. But it *is* a faith-informed one—because you can't talk about purity culture without talking about the religious systems that built it.

I don't go to church anymore. Sometimes I miss it—until I try to go back and leave angrier than I arrived. I just can't sit calmly at tables meant to be flipped.

I no longer claim Christianity, because I believe its institutions have caused more harm than healing. The receipts are endless—colonization, crusades, queerphobia, abuse coverups, purity culture. Still, I think Jesus was a bold, non-white radical guy worth learning from. So I've just put my faith in Love instead. And She has never let me down.

You might still be in church. You might be deconstructing. You might be completely done. You're welcome here, exactly as you are.

This book is *hard on systems and soft on people.* I will name the harm—but I will never shame your journey. I'll be honest about the damage religion can cause, and I'll honor whatever parts of your faith you still want to keep.

Purity culture tried to take away your agency. I won't do that. You get to decide what to hold and what to release.

Grab my hand—we're jumping in. I'll go first.

Chapter 1: Twenty-Six-Year-Old Virgin Turned Sex Expert

See this delighted bride? This is me. I'm leaving my dreamy morning wedding with the man I adored and loved. Moments later, I had full-on "tab A into slot B" sex for the very first time—only to find out that my vagina was painfully broken. Little did I know that this first-time fiasco would eventually sprout my career as a sexologist.

When we reached our hotel room, my newly minted husband, Nathan, oh so tenderly helped extract me from my eBay wedding dress, clip-in hair extension, fake eyelashes, full-body Spanx, and two sticky chicken cutlets also known as a strapless, backless bra.

By this time, I half-expected to glance up to find New Husband on the phone with his lawyer, chicken cutlet in his palm, discussing what to do about a bait-and-switch. Instead, like a true gentleman, he simply smiled reassuringly and handed me a glass of champagne.

I will spare you the details of losing my "virginity." The end result was me lying "all black mascara weepy" and discouraged in luxurious Egyptian cotton sheets. What was supposed to have been an incredibly pleasurable and intimate first-time, all-out sex experience felt more like a hysterectomy without anesthesia. I'd been under the impression that my valiant effort to remain a virgin until marriage would guarantee phenomenal, mind-blowing, heart-throbbing sex.

No? Apparently, "prosperity gospel," especially when it comes to sex, is problematic.

I remember strolling around Austin later that day, thinking, *My vagina still hurts. This was not how I thought sex was supposed to feel. I waited twenty-six years . . . for this? Maybe I waited too long. Are my lady parts just . . . old and rusty? Surely this was just a first-time kinda thing. Surely it will get better with a few more rounds.*

It didn't.

Our honeymoon *was* amazing, except for the awful sex. We continued the theme of painful sex throughout our first year of marriage, awkwardly trying to sorta fix it and also never talk about it. During that first year, we moved 742 miles away from our beloved

Texas, and everything familiar, to Missouri, where New Husband could start medical school. The sex was so incredibly painful, and it resulted in me experiencing resentment, anger, sexual shame, and low libido. Yay! If you have ever been freshly married, you probably understand that freshly marrieds have no concept of how to handle such things.

Eventually, any time New Husband reached out to me physically, simply trying to connect, I would cringe and avoid as simmering anger bubbled under the surface of my delicate skin. I was angry at myself for being naïve enough to think sex would be amazing *because* I waited; angry (wrongly) at him for not having all the solutions and not fixing it; and angry at a God who would allow me to suffer at the hands of a church community that refused to give me the language to reach out for help.

I then showed up for every other part of my life in spades, trying to make up for the intense loss and loneliness I felt in my sex life. I took on the role of primary financial provider by teaching at the local university as an adjunct professor, being a graduate assistant, tutoring a second grader after work, and cleaning horse stalls on the weekends. I also continued to fly back to Texas one weekend a month to continue work on my PhD. I took care of our house, tried my best to make meals, and religiously walked our sweet lab, Stevie Ray, every night.

Because I felt like a failure between the sheets, I was determined to be the perfect spouse in every other way. The funny thing is that no matter how perfect my house, my teaching, or my dog walking, I continued to feel angry and anxious about sex.

I learned later that painful sex is common in women. But I didn't learn that until much later. And, as in my experience, it often leads to resentment, low libido, and sexual shutdown. There are many things you can do—behaviorally—to combat these issues.

But during our first year of marriage, I felt there were no options. I felt like a complete and total failure as a wife.

One year later, when I was back in Texas for a summer course, I scheduled an appointment with an ob-gyn. I showed up in the waiting room nervous but hopeful that this guy would have some very specific answers and treatments. He did what I thought was a very thorough examination. I waited patiently.

Following his assessment, the doctor explained, "You know, Celeste, I can't see anything physical that would cause your sexual discomfort. I think this pain will probably go away once you have your first vaginal birth."

What the *actual* fuck?

At the time, I didn't even want kids. Nor was I having any kind of sex that would create a human life in my uterus. Most importantly, I needed so much more than a well-stretched vagina.

I needed somebody with more sexual knowledge to look me straight in the eye and say, "Celeste, you are not broken. Celeste, I see that you are hurting. Your pain and anger are valid. Celeste, we are going to walk this road together until you are all the way free."

I needed somebody to say that painful sex is common but can get better with some intentional behaviors. I needed somebody to hold my hand and empathize with how the fabric of my new marriage was getting thin and how I was scared that we would never recover from my resentment and anger. I needed to hear that my pleasure was important too and that my sexual experience could be broadened to include all kinds of sexual experiences—and *not* the painful ones. I needed someone to just *see* me in my pain and struggle.

Instead, this professional's suggestion for ending my painful sex was . . . to get pregnant?

Had I not been spread eagle on the exam table, I might have pecked the physician down onto the cold tile with his own speculum. But I *was* spread eagle. And young, naïve, and timid. So instead, I mumbled something close to "Oh, okay. Well . . . okay" and laid my head back on the exam table in defeat as the paper crinkled beneath me.

As the moments passed though, this was when a tiny but resolute, fiery-hot ember sparked. That was the moment when the plot of my sex life rerouted and my career path sprouted. I stopped waiting for someone to hand me the keys to a lock they didn't understand or sign a permission slip for my own pleasure.

At that moment, I started the journey of becoming the professional I needed. I had to let go of any preconceived notions about what good sex looks like and create, from scratch, my own version of good sex.

Driving home, I thought about all the advice I'd taken about sex up until that moment. "Wait until marriage. Save yourself for somebody special. Don't cause a man to lust after you with how you dress. Don't get too physical because that might cause you to stumble. If you stumble, ask for forgiveness. Go and *sin* no more."

My sexual choices up until that point had been largely based on what others expected of me. I am a born rule-follower because that's how I feel *safe*. I had waited to have sex until I was married, largely because that was what my community expected of me. That was the rule, and I didn't ask why—I just knew I felt safer following the rule. The implicit message I received while growing up in my community was that sex was unsafe. Follow the rules, and you will never feel pain or be unsafe. Right?

Now that I was married, I was trying to force myself to live by the rules of what I thought sex should look like based on what little I had learned from society. I was following the rules of society's "sex," so I figured I should be feeling safe in my relationship, right?

Nope. All I received by conforming to these standards was physical pain, the feeling that I was a fraud, and emotional shame for not living up.

The interesting thing about our bodies is that they are super smart. And they *remember*. My body remembered millions of times I'd been told all the different ways that sex was *unsafe*. That if I did it, I'd get an STI or a pregnancy. And, worst of all, I would be committing a *sin*. I'd go to hell! (Hell sounds super unsafe.)

I had always, always, always followed the "rules." I'd never questioned, never explored, and never gotten hurt. This was how I'd felt safe for so long. But now I was over it. Done. I was finished allowing these messages to influence the most intimate parts of my life. I was over not being my own advocate and not speaking up.

With this little spark of agency—of taking back my own sex life and making it mine—I decided to try again. Being the nerd I was, I decided to go back into sex with the intention of collecting data. I wanted to start from neutral. But Nathan and I were both hesitant. This part of our lives had delivered me such pain. However, this time, there were no fake eyelashes and no Spanx. There were no high expectations and no champagne. There were just two people who were hoping for something better and a little more knowledgeable. We were a bit more tender. And a lot more clear.

And the sex was . . . drumroll, please . . . still quite painful. But there was a hint of a difference. Something had morphed within me. I no longer felt such resentment toward Nathan. I felt the anger dissipate into curiosity. Sex education books started to clutter my nightstand. I was devouring information. If I was willing to get vulnerable enough to read everything I could about sex, what else could I be willing to try? I slowly began to bump up against the old ideas I had in my head about what sex was *supposed* to be. Even more slowly, those old, dusty ideas started to fall away, and I began to discover what I wanted sex to look like for me. And for us.

I learned how to touch my own body in sex, how to self-soothe, and how to seek safety within my own skin. I kept telling myself that pleasure was safe.

We kept trying, and we kept evolving. And we talked about what we were learning. We discussed what was pleasant and what was just meh.

I began to rebuild my sexual confidence. I figured out that I had to have good emotions about sexual touch before I could have good sensations during sensual touch. We had gotten into a negative feedback loop in which he would reach out to connect physically, and I would withdraw. So he would feel rejected and stop reaching out. Then I would feel rejected. We were circling and circling.

Eventually, I realized this and decided to work to stop the cycle on my end. The only way I'd ever be okay with penetrative sex again was to start being okay with sexual touch. And the only way I'd be okay with sexual touch was if I knew, beyond a shadow of a doubt, that sexual touch would not hurt. So it took a hard conversation about boundaries and a lot of work on both our parts to stick to sexual activities that were not penetrative and therefore felt good or at least neutral.

I also worked on my thoughts and ideas about sex. I became more aware of where my ideas about sex were coming from. I unpacked the messages I'd been given throughout my life and systematically and slowly started to reject the messages that were untrue or came primarily from the male gaze.

Once I started understanding and rejecting where my negative messages came from, I began to honor my need for better sex education.

I was getting a PhD in health education, and I was learning all about people's behaviors, why we do what we do, and how our choices are formed. Environment, social status, race, gender, and income are all involved in creating our behaviors. The more I learned about our health behaviors, the more I could apply it to sexual behaviors. *My* sexual behaviors.

Why do people eat the way they eat? Or exercise the way they exercise? Well, turns out it has a lot to do with the environment they are in, how much knowledge they have about food or exercise, what their culture says about food and movement, and how accessible food and movement are. Wouldn't this apply to sexual behaviors too? Why do people have sex the way they have sex? It probably has a lot to do with environment, culture, knowledge, and accessibility.

Why does everyone think it's okay to have all this conversation and education about every behavior except for sex? I wondered. *That's so weird.*

I understood the makeup of my sexual messaging. I honored my need for comprehensive sex education. Then I created behaviors that broke negative feedback loops.

Shame was next on the list. I worked on demolishing shame by bringing it into the light. I was ashamed of being "less than" what I thought I should be sexually, but when I brought it into the light, I was able to give myself compassion. How was I supposed to feel empowered and unashamed when my whole life had been about avoiding sex because it was seen as disempowering?

Compassion, compassion, compassion.

I got really clear on what I wanted to feel during sex, not just on what I wanted to do. The emotions of sex were the core motivator behind what happened, so I sought out clarity there. I wanted to feel light, fun, seen, valid, pleasured, and connected. I understood what Nathan wanted to feel too: desired, loved, and connected. We were rooting into our five senses during sex, and we honored each other's needs, wants, and boundaries. We stumbled, broke boundaries, went backward, and got clear again. We moved forward.

It was not easy.

Being aware of messages, gaining comprehensive sex knowledge, rejecting limiting beliefs, honoring turn-ons and turn-offs, demolishing shame through compassion, and finally seeking pleasure as an experience helped pave a path to liberation. I will tell you how to do everything I learned in the upcoming chapters.

The more I sought out pleasure with Nathan as an experience without penetration as a goal, the more pleasure I experienced. And the more liberated any sexual experience was.

I felt the plaster cast of my limited sexuality cracking. My "head back, eyes closed, mouth open" sexual experiences were freeing me.

I resiliently continued to step into vulnerability. Courage over comfort.

In our second year of marriage, I had penetrative sex for the first time without anxiety *or* pain. It was like my entire intimate world had finally broken open. I was experiencing new pleasure and connection. But honestly, it actually happened way before the penetration. The *journey* to discovering my own sexual story had powerfully matured me and my relationship, connecting us in ways that would have never happened had I not struggled so profoundly.

Following this first new sexual experience, I was again black-mascara weepy. But this time, I was weepy with joy, love, confidence, and hope.

Part 1:
The Analyst

Awareness is the greatest agent for change.[1]

The Analyst inside you will do the work of awareness. She is the part of you who is curious, skeptical, and data-driven. She asks, "Where did I learn this, and is it actually true?"

She helps you:

- Identify inherited sexual scripts
- Notice internal contradictions
- Track patterns of thought, behavior, and shame
- Hold space for discomfort without rushing to fix it

Her tools are reflection, observation, and inquiry. She doesn't jump to conclusions—she gathers information. She's the inner researcher, the sex-ed messaging sleuth, and the intake nurse with a clipboard.

Her power lies in compassionate awareness. Because when you name something, you can change it.

Chapter 2: What Is In Your Backpack?

In 2017, Nate and I hiked sixteen miles in the Grand Tetons. Our goal? Spot bears and moose, of course! We loaded up our backpacks, and off we went. But, I ended up staring at my feet the entire time because my pack was just too heavy. Like a total newbie, I'd crammed in a journal (that I never touched), a giant camera (that I barely used), and a family-size roll of toilet paper (did I think I was going to poo the whole time?). By the end, I realized I'd spent more time thinking about my aching shoulders than enjoying the trail or spotting anything furry.

Back at the condo that evening (yes, with running water—I'm not that hardcore), I wanted to thoughtfully consider what I would take on the next day's hike. If my goal was to take in the scenery, I needed to assess what was keeping my shoulders sore and eyes down. I liberated the contents of my bag and started sorting.

Water? Essential. I'd absolutely need that.

Bear spray? Also essential. Not because I'd absolutely have to use it but because it was a required safety net. I'd have to carry it no matter what.

The rest? Not so much. I tossed the journal, toilet paper, and DSLR camera onto the couch. Unnecessary and heavy, they were keeping me from seeing the wildlife.

The next day, with a lighter pack, I finally looked up from the path. That's when I saw a moose.

The moral? Before tackling anything hard, take off your backpack and see what you're really carrying. You might be surprised at how much lighter you feel when you ditch the stuff you don't actually need.

What are you carrying? What is in your backpack?

We are all given a backpack at birth. As we age, our backpack fills up with messages, ideas, and value systems. Before we become adults, parents, experiences, culture, and traumatic events place most of these messages into our backpacks for us. Many of those messages are loving, kind, helpful, and needed:

- Look both ways before crossing the road.
- Always wash your hands.
- Mama will always be here to listen.
- You are such a hardworking kiddo.
- You can do anything you set your mind to!

Other messages are helpful for a time:

- Don't watch scary movies until your brain is able to decipher fact from fiction.
- Don't ride with someone you don't know.

And still others are harmful right from the beginning:

- Children are to be seen and not heard.
- Your genitals are nasty. Don't touch them.
- If you loved me, you would let me touch you there.

Some messages work their way out of the backpack naturally. (What? No tooth fairy?) Most messages must be assessed intentionally. When we don't, we end up carrying way too much for far too long.

Because sex has been exceptionally difficult to talk about, the messages we get in our pack when we're growing up don't often get questioned. (Like the tooth fairy does.) Because sex remains mysterious and dark, the messages simmer and get heavier.

Other packs we carry, like the religion backpack, are checked a bit more regularly because looking into what we believe about God and church and theology is common and, in many ways, encouraged (thankfully) in most church settings. Think about what you learned about God and religion as a young person and what you believe about God and religion now. Are they different? I hope so. That is because, at some point, you took off the religion backpack and took a peek inside.

By the time a client comes to see me, her pack typically contains fifty pounds of sexual bullshit. It's too overwhelming to look into it on her own anymore. She needs permission *just to set it down.*

The enlightened hiker stops, sits down, and analyzes her pack. She examines what's inside to identify the unnecessary, heavy ideas about sex that she wants to leave behind. Now she can take a deep breath and take in the view. The possibilities. The expansiveness and beauty. She can decide for herself what she wants sex to be. Now she knows what she was carrying. And she can address what she wants to consciously bring with her on her journey and what she wants to leave behind.

Activity: Sex Is . . . and Dream Sex Would Feel Like . . .

Here is a great activity to start you out. This is your Analyst understanding where her sex life is currently and where she wants it to be in the future. In the Tetons, I started in the parking lot. But I wanted to experience the joy of seeing animals on the trail. I couldn't make a plan until I knew those two things.

Take a paper and draw a line down the middle. On one half of the paper, write the heading "Sex is . . ." On the other half of the paper, write the heading "My dream sexual experience would be . . ."

Give yourself two minutes on your phone timer and put your phone on Do Not Disturb mode. For the next two minutes, write down every adjective, phrase, or feeling that describes how sex is for you currently. This is not what you want for the future— these are just simple descriptions of what sex is for you right now. Try to manage any judgment that arises. Just let the words flow. You may find that some of your words even contradict each other. That's okay too. Just write.

After those two minutes are over, take a deep breath, stretch, and set your timer for two more minutes. Spend two minutes in your second column, writing down every adjective, phrase, feeling, or behavior that describes your dream sexual experience. I say, "dream sexual experience" instead of just "sex" because I want you to think more broadly about sex. It's not just penetration or orgasm. It's everything, from the moment you start thinking about sex with your partner to the moment you are falling asleep or getting dressed. You may find that you have contradictory words in here too. That's totally okay.

Here is an example of what it might look like:

Sex is...	My dream sexual experience would be...
A chore	Passionate
Painful	Pleasurable
Loving and good for my relationship	Connective
Something I avoid	Intimate
Intimate	Good for our relationship
Sometimes feels good	Desired

Once you have your two lists, see if there are any similarities between them. Are there any differences? This activity is vitally important in helping you figure out how to get from where you are to where you want to go. It can be difficult to make changes in any aspect of your life if you don't know how you feel now and how you want to feel.

As you look on your list, focus on anything you wrote down that is an emotion because we are motivated to behave in order to feel certain things. For example, I don't particularly love running, but I run because I like the feeling it gives me. I eat delicious food not because I like chewing but because I like the taste of the food.

Once you know where you are and where you want to be, you can discover the messages that create the behaviors that keep you from getting from here to there. In the next section, you will discover the intense dichotomous messages of purity culture and the explicit patriarchal culture, as well as why we don't actually align with either of them.

Chapter 3: Me in the Middle

Hands to heaven, this entire story is absolute truth.

After being married for three years, I secured a job as the head of the sexual health education department at a sex toy company. Part of this very fascinating job was assisting with product purchasing and development. That involved ensuring that the products were both safe and appealing to the target customer.

If there is one thing I know way too much about, it is sex toys.

I have learned a lot *from* sex toys too. Sex Toy Company once decided to do a product rollout at a convention center ballroom with a packed live audience of company sales representatives. One of my duties (per se) at this event was to manage a gaggle of six male models who were adorned in only thongs, leather chaps, and cowboy hats. I was to make sure they were in proper costume.

Then I was to give them each a silver tray piled high with our new dildo, which was called Cowboy Up.

The pinnacle of this chore was to usher the models from the dressing room and through the lobby of the convention hotel to Ballroom A, where they would proceed to hand out free dildos, just like Oprah. After I reluctantly lent a helping hand to gorgeous Chaz and Damian (who had a combined age of my actual age—absolute fetuses, really) with their leather chap costume malfunctions, we were ready to roll. Everyone outfitted, trays of dildos lifted high, we started our breathtakingly good-looking trek across the lobby.

Right before we walked out, I imagined how we would appear: *The green room door flings open. Yours Truly emerges with six hot fellas slo-mo walking behind me in a V formation. I'm their leading lady, confidently escorting them in my androgynous blue pantsuit and sensible flats. Beyoncé's "Diva" is dropping hard in the background.*

There I was, in all my feminist glory, escorting six freshly waxed male models who were holding silver trays covered with dildos.

But when I threw open the door, all I saw was a *holy sea of priests* in full-blown albs, waiting magnanimously to enter their own priest-y event in the other ballroom.

Beyoncé stopped singing.

You know, there are moments in life when time stands still: enjoying that first embrace of your newborn . . . conquering that marathon . . . escorting scantily clad and barely legal male models through a priest convention. These are the universal moments many people experience, when one stops and acknowledges, "I am *really* alive. This is what living is, and I have reached the apex of all life has to offer. If I survive this, I can die happy and never have any regrets."

At twenty-seven years of life, crossing that lobby was my Everest.

As it turns out, both of my shirtless, chest-hairless friends and my ecclesiastical comrades were cordial, if not downright friendly, as we passed each other in the lobby. All fell silent. The fetuses nodded respectfully, chests out, lips pursed, and nipples erect, dropping nary a dildo. The priests, seeing the determined (shall I say, sanctified?) journey we were on, parted like the Red Sea and ushered us through. A couple of them even gestured with their noble wizard-like arms to the best direction for our safe passage.

Still, nobody spoke. (I can't speak on behalf of the silent prayers, though. I had a few thousand of my own.) It was like the most bizarre lunar eclipse that happens once every 423 years. The culmination of timing, richness of characters, and immaculate juxtaposition of costume design could have won us all Emmys. It was amazing.

This apotheosis experience of seeing sexiness and holiness divided into distinct camps reminds me of the two buckets that society wants women to stay in. On one side is overt sexuality—the assless chaps and stacks of dildos. On the other side is holy, pure *religion*.

And then there was me. In the middle. With my prayers, my sensible flats, my dildos, and my job at a sex toy company.

The work of sexual reclamation is to help you break rank on either side and embrace the *and* of the middle. When we are told that we must be *either*, we are minimized as people. And as women. When we are told that we must be sexual *or* sanctified, the complexity of our humanness begins to be erased.

When you live in only one or the other bucket, you start ceasing to exist. But the power of *and* brings you back to life:

- I can hitch, drive, and haul a six-horse trailer, *and* I'd rather have my husband do it.
- I am unsure about my body, *and* I feel confident in it.
- I struggle with reading, *and* I have earned a PhD.
- I teach women how to orgasm, *and* I think Jesus is pretty cool.
- I am a vegetarian, *and* I support non-trophy hunting.

The prohibitive buckets of patriarchal exploitative sex and purity culture are lies. You can't actually live all in one or all in the other. Nobody does. But we are told to at least pretend that we do. And if we talk about how we don't, we are shamed for being out of line.

I can assure you that priests have sexual thoughts. And I can also assure you that those male models have said a prayer or two. This is the power of *and*. We can be both sexual *and* divine.

In your Analyst mode, look for the buckets and how they have been defined for you in your life. They are black or white. But life and sex begin to fully reveal themselves to you when you embrace your *and* by stepping out of black or white and into the middle.

Which, for the record, is not gray.

It is glitter.

The Glitter Area

"That's a gray area." That phrase used to describe areas of our lives that are nondescript, foggy, or unclear. The gray area isn't a sure thing. We may not be able to count on the boundaries to hold us together. The gray areas are the shades of truth that remain between the extremes.

There are very few areas of life that have more extreme ends than sex: the white bucket of purity culture on one side and the black bucket of exploitative sex on the other. The world would make us think that we hop from one bucket to the other. In high school, you were a prude until you had sex. Then you were a slut. You are to be "good" until you sign a marriage certificate, and then you are to be a "vixen."

A lady on the street and a freak in the bed?

Being between those two buckets is difficult, though. It is hard to talk about sex when we can't define it as ruthlessly pure or evil. The gray area seems hard to stay in because the confinement of the buckets is comforting. Compliance with a strong border is easy. We like the security of walls because they keep us safe from the outside—until the walls keep us from experiencing the outside at all.

Brené Brown calls this area the wilderness:

> Wilderness—an untamed, unpredictable place of solitude and searching. It is a place as dangerous as it is breathtaking, a place as sought after as it is feared. The wilderness can often feel unholy because we can't control it, or what people think about our choice of whether to venture into that vastness or not. But it turns out to be the place of true belonging, and it's the bravest and most sacred place you will ever stand.[2]

Most of us find ourselves longing to step out of one or the other bucket in our sex lives. We don't fit the confined walls of purity or exploitative sexuality. The middle is difficult. Brené uses the term *the wilderness*, but I am going to use the term *glitter*. When we step out of our black and white buckets, we land not in gray and not in wilderness. We land in glitter! Which is sparkly and joyful and fun!

If you have ever had glitter inside your house, you know that glitter isn't always wonderful. See also: messy, frustrating, everlasting, and difficult to control.

That is the point.

I want your sex life to feel like glitter. Joyful and messy and difficult and fun. Just when you think you have it under control, you have another kid or a change in career or an endometriosis diagnosis, and you realize that the glitter cannot be contained to one area. Your sex life is affected by and affects your environment and your circumstances. It is constantly shifting.

You belong in the glitter. Nobody really truly belongs in the buckets, but everyone is told they do. The glitter is where you will find the relationship to sex that is truly yours. It is authentic and hard. Be brave and step out of the buckets of limited sexuality, then join me in the glitter. Once you do, there is no going back.

Activity: Awareness of the Dichotomy

Society tells us that there are two lanes of sexuality and that we "should" stick to one lane. On one side is explicit sexuality: a free-for-all, no-consequences kind of approach to sex. On the other side is purity culture: a highly controlling, fear-based approach to sex in the name of Christianity.

The Analyst within you is setting down her heavy pack and is now ready to notice the ways sex has been polarized in your own life. Of course, this will look similar in many ways for a lot of people, and it will look different in a lot of ways too. But most importantly, this is *your* backpack. Nobody else has one like yours.

Here is a writing activity for this awareness practice. On a piece of paper, create a line down the middle of a page. At the top of the left side, write "Exploitive Sexual Culture." At the top of the right side, write "Controlling Purity Culture." Give yourself five minutes for each side and write down how you have experienced pressure to conform to each bucket. Here are some examples from my life:

Exploitive Sexual Culture	Controlling Purity Culture
Magazines that indicate sexy = very little clothes and a thin body with big, perky boobs.	Being told I will be a half-eaten brownie if I have any sexual touch/experiences before marriage.
Pornography says sex is easy for everyone and that if you don't want it all the time, something is wrong with you	Being told sex is so profound that I am "soul tied" forever to whoever puts their penis inside my vagina.
Men want and think about sex uncontrollably and constantly. It is your job to please him.	Men want and think about sex uncontrollably and constantly. It is your job to keep him from sinning.

The polarization of really anything is simply a lot of lies on either side of the spectrum. It is difficult to know why we feel so badly about ourselves until we begin to see the lies we have been told to conform to. When we try to conform to the lies, we inevitably fail. And we feel like failures. What is authentic and true is in the middle of the spectrum. But we would never have known that without knowing what's on the end of each side of the scale.

Notice. Notice. Notice.

Next, underneath your two columns, try writing down what actually feels true for you about a few of your statements. You may not know what feels true yet because you are in the beginning stages of sexual becoming. But you may have a few ideas.

When you write down something true, notice what happens in your body. Does it settle? Does it get excited? Do you feel confident? Begin to home in on the feeling of authenticity. Even if there are just the tiniest changes in your body or energy, notice them. The better you get at noticing those tiny changes when you speak the truth, the better you will get at knowing what you want in sex and in life. When authenticity shows up, your body will know, and vice versa. Your body (and I believe Spirit) will always attempt to lead you there. All you have to do is put down the pack and notice.

Notice, notice, notice.

Here are some authentic truths that came up for me after I wrote about the polarization of sexual messages:

- Sexy is an attitude and has a lot to do with confidence.
- It's okay if I don't want to have sex all the time. That makes me human.
- It is not my responsibility or job to please my partner or manage my partner's behaviors.
- I get to define sex. For me, it includes many behaviors that aren't penetrative.

In the next chapter, you will learn about a way to organize sex that functions much better than the buckets.

Chapter 4: The Sexual Hierarchy of Needs

When I first started out as a sex educator, I found it frustrating that we didn't have a very good framework with which to talk about *healthy* sex. Women and couples were coming in with harmful messages that were messing up their sex lives, and I wanted to be able to describe a healthy version of sex, not just dissect the unhealthy parts.

There were theories about how sex happens in the body, like the sexual response cycle[3] by Masters and Johnson, and descriptions of where dysfunction may have started in childhood, such as Freud's five stages of psychosexual development.[4] (Side note: Freud's theories did a *lot* of damage to women—damage we still deal with today. I'm not a fan.) But these were not comprehensive descriptions of how to understand and navigate healthy sexuality.

I wanted even more clarity. Clients needed to know why they were struggling, what to do about it specifically, and in what order to do the steps. In many areas of behavior, order matters.

For example, if I'm helping a woman find less disgust surrounding her genitals, I start by helping her learn to say the anatomical names—clitoris, labia, vulva, etc. When she is comfortable there, we get curious about her ability to look at her own vulva. When she is comfortable there, we move to have her touch her vulva.

When she says she finds her genitalia disgusting, it would make zero sense to ask her to go to her local sex toy store to buy and start using a vibrator and *then* teach her how to comfortably say *clitoris*. In fact, this might even be activating or traumatizing.

Order *matters*. By and large, I found psychological theories convoluted and hard to relate to in a practical way in the bedroom. Health education theories that worked well for smoking cessation or seat-belt compliance fell flat in an area that nobody felt comfortable talking about. This irked me because we had to have better ways to understand a healthy, functioning sex life if we wanted to help people change the way they view sex or behave in a sexual experience. If we didn't have that, we couldn't understand what can go wrong. So I set out to find a clearer and more organized way to explain the concept of sex and what we need in our sex lives in order to help our sex lives survive and thrive.

When I dug into some of my textbooks from my health education background, I began to look through theories that could organize sexual experiences in a way that made more practical sense. I don't want to bore you with the details of trying to apply health behavior change theories to sex, but the result was extraordinary. I rediscovered Maslow's hierarchy of needs[5] and thought about how simple and straightforward it is.

Bingo.

We typically learn about Maslow's hierarchy of needs in basic psychology classes. It is one of the primary theories, and it can be applied to every human on Earth. For the record, Maslow borrowed heavily from the Blackfoot Nation model of communal thriving and self-actualization, stripped it of its collective spirit, repackaged it as an individualistic ladder to success, and never gave them credit. That's a shitty thing to do.

This hierarchy is in the shape of a pyramid and has five levels. Essentially, the bottom level is what it takes to survive the next minute or the next hour or the next day. As you are fulfilled in each level, you can move to the next. The first two levels are primarily physical needs, and the last three levels are emotional needs.

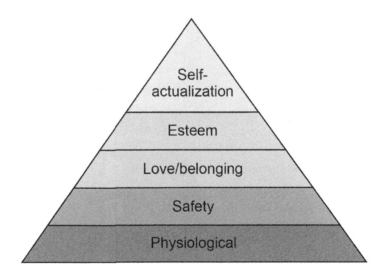

I decided to take Maslow's (appropriated from the Blackfoot Nation) hierarchy of needs and use it in my sexology practice. Ladies and gentlemen, gays and theys: the Sexual Hierarchy of Needs. I placed the filter of sex over Maslow's pyramid, and it organized sex in a practical way that makes sense and creates order. It can help people understand where they are struggling while also giving individual freedom in figuring out what behaviors can lead them forward.

The Sexual Hierarchy of Needs places sexual experiences in the order of how we need to receive them to feel sexually fulfilled at the top. The order of physiology first, safety and consent second, love and belonging third, and pleasure fourth leads to sexual actualization and agency. We often get stuck in a single layer, and sexual progress becomes stagnant.

Sexual Hierarchy of Needs
by Celeste Holbrook, Ph.D

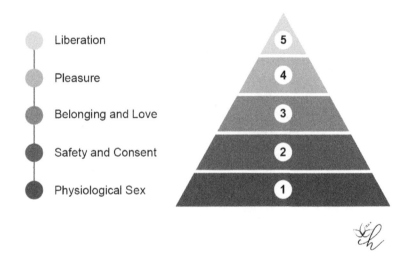

- Liberation — 5
- Pleasure — 4
- Belonging and Love — 3
- Safety and Consent — 2
- Physiological Sex — 1

This was my road into sexual discernment through the lens of science. I had finally found a way to describe the sequence of healthy sexuality, from physical needs to emotional needs. I was thrilled.

We are going to take a look at the Sexual Hierarchy of Needs to learn how healthy sexuality builds. It's a best practice in science.

Physiological Layer of the Sexual Hierarchy of Needs

At the bottom of Abraham Maslow's hierarchy of needs, we find all of our biological needs, which are the elements we require in order to live to the next minute, the next hour, and the next few days. These necessities include air, food, and water. We must have these to simply exist. Descartes might have said, "I think therefore I am," but I'm sure he was also drinking water and eating food. Once we have these needs fulfilled, we can go up one rung on the ladder.

When we place the filter of sexuality over this foundational layer, we create the first level of the Sexual Hierarchy of Needs. This is where we find all the physiological ways one would describe sex— the positions, acts, biology, anatomy, and physiological responses. I challenge you to think about how you personally define sex. What goes into this foundational layer for you?

As we described earlier, sex is often defined for us through religious organizations, family systems, or even the media. But how would you define it? Many people define sex as a penis inserted into a vagina. But this becomes problematic when two partners maybe don't have penises at all. Or what if one partner doesn't get an erection anymore and can't be inserted into a vagina? What if one partner experiences painful penetration? Does this mean the end of sex? I would love for you to start defining sex and all the physiological stuff that happens in this foundational layer. Make wide, sweeping, inclusive descriptions of what sex is physiologically.

It could be naked skin touching naked skin. Or it could be vulvas rubbing together. Or mouth and vulva touching. Or penis and anus. Or penis and ear . . . It could be two people grinding with their clothes on. It could be two partners describing sex acts to each other over FaceTime. It could be a lot of different things.

The more you can expand the way you describe physical sex, the more inclusive your world will become. And the easier it will be to enjoy sexual experiences because so many more behaviors might be included. (There are no right or wrong answers here. You get to define sex for yourself. So include as many as possible.)

The way you define sex physically is in the very first layer of the Sexual Hierarchy of Needs. You cannot experience the other layers unless you know how to define sex for you.

This physiological layer of sex is so important because you need to know quite a bit about your own body before you can give informed consent to a partner. Consent is valid only when it is informed.

This is why comprehensive sex ed is so important. Understanding sex in a very physical way and understanding how to define sex broadly is vitally important in helping our young people establish healthy sexual behaviors. When our kids don't understand how to define sex, it becomes very difficult, or even impossible, to give and receive informed consent. The thing about informed consent is that it is *informed*. As in *educated*. As in *comprehensive*. I get a little fired up about this subject.

When we don't provide comprehensive sex ed, kids end up getting into scenarios they know *nothing* about. So they can't give informed consent. They can give only consent without knowledge, education, or information. Which is *not consent*.

Comprehensive sex ed is a prerequisite for informed, consensual sex.

Understanding your body so you can truly give informed consent (the next layer) and experience high sensual self-esteem, arousal, pleasure, and worth *all* begins with fully understanding your body and sex. And all of this has to begin with comprehensive sex education, which is the physiological foundation.

Consent and Safety Layer of the Sexual Hierarchy of Needs

The next level is safety and consent. Safety can be both a physical, tangible thing, like a house to sleep in. Or it can be a social construct, like a community that works to keep you safe. In sex, one clear example of safety is protecting yourself from unwanted pregnancy and sexually transmitted infections. Or having sex in a safe place with a safe partner.

This layer also includes sexual trust and how to give and receive informed consent. Please note that this layer is *before* pleasure and sexual agency. Safety is required in order to feel aroused.

The body is built to react to threats with a fight, flight, freeze, or fawn response. We will talk more about this later in the book. But just know that the body often has the same fear response to perceived threats that it would have to an actual lion in the jungle. Now imagine that your body got the message from a young age that sex = danger (such as going to hell, getting STIs, or not belonging). If the body perceives sex as unsafe, there will be no climbing up the pyramid. It will shut down any nonessential systems (like arousal) so it can move into its fear response (which, in this case, is often freeze). The sexual experience basically ends before you ever feel pleasure, belonging, or connection.

How can I say this more clearly? The messages from purity culture told you that sex is "dangerous." Now you may be having a hard time finding sex pleasurable because your body doesn't feel safe.

This layer is where many women who grew up in purity culture struggle. They wonder why they don't desire sex, don't feel aroused, have painful sex, etc. It turns out that it begins with understanding that the body feels sex is unsafe.

Add to purity culture the lived experience of just being a woman in this society—which is an unsafe existence in general—and you'll see that half the population is in an almost constant state of elevated awareness, hypervigilance, and fear response in their bodies.

Elevated awareness and hypervigilance translate into a wandering mind, an inability to be present, and a constant thought train about everything but sex when you *really* want to be enjoying sex.

No wonder sex is difficult to want.

Fortunately, when you do feel safe in a sexual scenario, you can give informed consent for sex acts. Then you move up another level to belonging and love. (As a side note, safe is not the same thing as known. You can feel safe with someone unknown or new—an element that's actually involved in *increasing* arousal.)

At this point, we have addressed only the elements we need to survive. Most of these have been physical needs. But if we have these elements in order, we can move up the hierarchy and discover the elements that we need to thrive, not just survive.

Sexual Belonging in the Sexual Hierarchy of Needs

On the third rung, we have emotional needs. These include the feeling of belonging and the idea of being loved. These are some of our most basic emotional needs. Keep in mind that these emotional needs are available to us only after our physical needs have been met. If I'm choking on a waffle, please do not tell me how much you love me. I need air first. Always.

Belonging and love? We know you can have great sex without feeling in love. And we know that you can be in love without having sex. But what about the belonging? Where does belonging fit into your sex life? Belonging is one of the most basic emotional needs. And it comes before love.

In education, we understand that kids need to have a healthy breakfast before they can concentrate or feel like they can belong in a classroom and subsequently learn well. In relationships, we have to feel safe before we feel like we belong. Although I'm not sure about Abraham Maslow's take, I believe that our most basic emotional need in life, not just in sex, is to belong. Even before being loved. We can spend a lot of our time feeling not loved. But if we feel like we don't belong, we will go to the ends of the Earth to find belonging. This is how people get involved in unhealthy social groups. The urge to feel like we belong somewhere is fierce. We desperately want to connect. We need to have people who want us.

Even if you may not feel like you belong in a relationship—like in a one-night stand, for example—I think it is important to feel like you *belong* in that particular sexual experience. You can choose to be sexually active with a stranger and feel physical pleasure in the absence of love as long as you feel like you belong there. I think it is important to feel embraced in that experience.

Belonging is foundational to love. Belonging doesn't need love, but love needs belonging. So belonging is the most basic emotional need in life in general and in our sex lives. Sometimes, you do love the person you're having sex with. I hope that you *do* have sex with someone you love someday if you haven't already. It's just that love is not required for great sex.

In a broader sense, belonging is also the feeling that sex is meant *for* you. However, many messages from purity culture and society keep women as a secondary piece of sex. The following messages are all examples of how we are indoctrinated to believe the idea that women don't belong in a sexual experience:

"He's a man. He just wants sex."

"Women are helpmates for men's pleasure."

"A woman's role is to make sure her man is satisfied."

"Men need sex every [insert quantity of time], and it is a woman's role to provide it."

"Two women having sex isn't really sex."

(Side note: Gag to all this bullshit. I hate even typing it.)

Sexual Esteem and Pleasure in the Sexual Hierarchy of Needs

If you go up one more layer in Maslow's hierarchy of needs, you will see esteem. This is when we feel like we are good at things. If our lower needs are met, we can more freely engage in behaviors, hobbies, communication, and other aspects of life with confidence. Thom is good at fixing motorcycles. Anita is fabulous at telling jokes. Shayla is a fantastic engineer. Julia helps people feel included. Darius is a stellar parent. These folks are thriving enough to feel confident in certain aspects of their lives.

When we shift to the Sexual Hierarchy of Needs, this layer is sexual esteem: confidence, self-worth, and a positive regard for your sexuality. This is the idea that you are good and worthy when it comes to sex. You don't have to be an experienced sexual expert to have confidence and think positively about your sexual experiences. In fact, you just need to have a strong foundation in the lower layers of the pyramid to have sexual esteem bloom.

You may find sexual esteem in the behaviors you engage in. Maybe you're good at initiating sex or receiving a bid for sex. Maybe you are great at listening and responding to your partner's needs. Maybe you are adept at blow jobs and masturbation. Maybe you're marvelous at strip teasing or silly sex or sex in nature. Regardless of what it is, you feel good at something in your sex life.

But even if you *don't* feel super confident in the behaviors of sex, you can feel positive about exploring and attempting them. This confident exploration and *willingness to find resilience* in failed attempts is highly discouraged in purity culture, which is obsessed with the traumatic concept of perfection. Purity culture wants us to believe in a sexual experience that is not learned but magically *known*. However, you and I know that when we tolerate the frustrating part of learning, confidence and resilience grow.

Along with esteem comes pleasure. Pleasure can be most deeply experienced when we are at the level of sexual esteem. You don't have to feel adept at every single thing you do sexually to feel pleasure. (If that were the case, none of us would be experiencing pleasurable sex.) But you do need to feel confident in the act of *trying*.

I find it fascinating that we identify sexual pleasure as being almost interchangeable with the idea of sex itself, even though pleasure doesn't even show up until almost the top of the pyramid. So that means you can know what to do physically, you can feel safe doing it, and you can even love the person you're doing it—but not feel pleasure. Specifically, sexual pleasure.

What does that mean?

That means that many clients are confounded by the fact that they love their partner, adore their relationship, and want to experience sexual pleasure. But they just . . . don't. This is confusing because purity culture tells us that if we wait until we love somebody and are committed to them, we'll experience good sex. It's the prosperity gospel of sex. If you behave in this certain way, pleasure is a given.

This is untrue. Sexual pleasure is not immediately granted just because you love somebody. Pleasure is your own responsibility. Not your partner's. Yours. And this balances delicately on the quality of your sex education and your feelings of safety and belonging.

Sexual Agency in the Sexual Hierarchy of Needs

At the very top of Maslow's pyramid, we have self-actualization, which, as a concept, can seem ethereal. So, let's break it down.

Self-actualization is really just the idea that we are in charge of how we react and respond to the world around us. When we take full ownership of how we react and respond, we can create a life that feels calm and fulfilling. It's not that bad things don't happen. It's just that we understand how to build the capacity to cope with them, how to get help when we need it, and how to take responsibility for our own actions.

The idea that pleasure is your own responsibility leads us to the top level in the Sexual Hierarchy of Needs: *sexual agency*. This is a way of understanding yourself that declares you are responsible for your reactions and your responses. Sexually. You get to be in charge of your own body, and you get to decide how to respond to sexual experiences.

Activity: Sexual Hierarchy of Needs Assessment

As you review the Sexual Hierarchy of Needs, which level do you feel you may get stuck in at times? Here are a few examples:

Kesha received the message that sex is something women provide for men. She has experienced low libido for most of her marriage. She subconsciously doesn't believe that sex is even for her. She is struggling in the area of *belonging*.

Becky has an ick factor when it comes to her partner's penis being on or in her. She has a very hard time with blow jobs and insists that her partner come in a towel away from her most of the time. Her disgust is with her own vulva, too, and she has never masturbated. When she was a young woman, her mother threatened to disown her if she ever got pregnant. Plus, she was routinely told not to touch her genitals. She feels fear when she thinks about genitalia because her education was rooted in danger. She is struggling in the layer of *safety*.

Tulip has been faking her orgasms for four years. It began with just a few times. But over the course of their relationship, her partner placed more and more pressure on her to orgasm because *he* loved it so much. When she just couldn't, he responded with frustration, asking her if she was even into him. In an attempt to protect herself from his fragility, she started to fake it. She is struggling in the layer of *safety*.

Rosalind hasn't ever touched herself or learned how to masturbate. Her family never talked about sex, and her Church told her that masturbation was wrong. Her lack of education and fear of nebulous consequences kept her from exploring. She knows very little about her vulva, clitoris, or vagina, and she has never had an orgasm. She is struggling in the *physiological/biological* layer.

Create a Sexual Hierarchy of Needs pyramid with some space where you can write a few notes about where you think you might be struggling. Remember: We aren't fixing anything per se. We are just becoming aware.

A note to those interested in a biblical view: I did a biblical study on the Song of Solomon as a best practice for sex, and the lovers (unmarried, I might add) are described as having achieved mastery in every level of the Sexual Hierarchy of Needs. I think this is the most beautiful example of a best practice for sex in the Bible.

Chapter 5: Sexual Ethic

My friend, you are worth more than the words and ideas of our fore*fathers*. You are worth more than their one-sided lens of sex. You are worth more than thousands of years of sex information being forced into your brain as truth in the guise of "purity" and "protection."

But what happens if you leave that behind? Many women want something different but voice a fear of the wild unknown outside purity culture. If they don't have the rigid rules of purity culture, will they have to accept every wild sex act that comes their way? In reality, all people have a sexual ethic, whether they grow up in church or not. A sexual ethic is a guide you use to make sexual decisions that are right for you.

You can change your trajectory and move away from shame and fear around sex. It doesn't have to define your sexual lens. I know it's possible because I did it. We do this by carefully questioning what we've learned and trying on a new worldview. Remember that sexual dysfunction comes from shame and lack of education. Sexual discernment is taking what you know about science, your values, and your inner voice, then blending it all to create a sexual ethic that works for you. When you are abiding by your *own* sexual ethic that is based on true sex education, shame dissipates. There is nothing to fear.

Do you know your sexual ethic? As in, how do you make your sexual choices? How do you know what you are and are not comfortable doing sexually? Have you ever thought about what informs the sexual choices you make?

One of my favorite ways to serve my community is to help women uncover their sexual ethic. Everyone has an ethic, but most of us don't spend time understanding how it is formed and whether it really serves our authentic self.

In short, I can help women establish their sexual ethic by looking at three main sources that inform how we make decisions about sex. These three constructs are sex education, intuition, and value systems. Developing yourself in these three areas is how you can create a sex ethic that is personal and unique to you.

Take a look at what *might* be included in each area:

Sex Education

- Comprehensive sex and pleasure education
- Understanding of pleasure anatomy
- Understanding of reproduction
- Consent discernment

Intuition

- What feels pleasurable
- What feels uncomfortable or painful
- Emotional intelligence
- Personal exploration

Value Systems

- Informed religious values
- Familial and cultural values
- Consent

In a healthy sexual ethic, all three of these categories play a role in balancing how you make sexual decisions. Unfortunately, many of us experience a lopsided approach to sexuality that is heavily influenced by one category: religion. This happens because we are not given the opportunity to have comprehensive sex education and our personal intuition about sex is not valued.

When you are making decisions about the sexual behaviors you want to try, I want you to check in with each of your sex ethic areas. I will give you an example using my own personal sex education ethic:

Sex education: I've got this down and am continuing to learn. ☺

Inner voice: A place you continue to check in with. Does my body and my brain want this?

Value system: There are three things in my value system construct—consent, pleasure, and monogamy. These three things must be present for me to have sex. If they aren't, I have sex outside my value system. Consent is the only one that must be present in *everybody's* ethic.

For example, if Jason Momoa shows up at my door and wants to have a threesome with me and Nate, here is how I would make that decision:

Sex education: Do I know how to navigate a threesome behaviorally? Probably yes. I have the skill sets and understanding needed to do this safely and emotionally educated.

Inner voice: Does a threesome with Jason Momoa and my husband sound great to my body and brain? Um, (cough) yes.

Value system: Is a threesome part of my value system? Nope. At this point in my life, I personally value monogamy for my own relationship, and so does my partner. So this idea is going to be a no for me and for him, even though it would check the other value system boxes of consent and pleasure.

See how you can use these constructs to make decisions about sexual exploration and behaviors. And can you also see how every person is going to have a different sex ethic based on their education, inner voice, and value system?

The goal isn't to have a "perfect" sexual ethic. It's to have one that's *conscious*. When you know what's in each of your three buckets—education, intuition, and values—you're not just reacting to situations. You're making choices that align with who you are. That's where sexual confidence lives. And the beauty of this framework is that it grows with you. As you learn more, feel more, and reflect more, your sexual ethic can evolve too. The point isn't to build rigid rules—it's to create a foundation you trust.

Activity: Build Your Sexual Ethic Buckets

Take a few minutes to reflect on each of the three areas. You can write full sentences, lists, or bullet points—whatever feels most natural. Be honest. Be kind. This isn't a test—it's a self-check-in.

1. Sexual Education and Knowledge

- What do I currently know about sexual anatomy, pleasure, consent, and reproduction?
- Where have I learned this from (school, media, books, experience)?
- Are there any gaps I'd like to fill in or topics I still have questions about?

2. Intuition (Inner Voice and Body Wisdom)

- What kinds of touch, situations, or experiences feel good to me?
- What has felt uncomfortable, disconnected, or painful (physically or emotionally)?
- How do I usually know when I'm a "yes" or a "no"?
- Do I feel safe listening to my body during sexual experiences?

3. Value Systems (Personal Beliefs and Boundaries)

- What values feel most important to me when it comes to sex (e.g., consent, honesty, pleasure, monogamy, sacredness, exploration)?
- Where did these values come from? Family, culture, religion, life experience?
- Are these still *my* values or ones I've inherited without reflection?

- What values must be present for me to feel good about a sexual experience?

Bonus Prompt

Try running a recent or hypothetical sexual scenario through your three buckets. Ask yourself:

- Do I have the knowledge or education for this?
- Do my body and brain want this?
- Does this align with my values?

You don't need all three to be screaming *yes* every time. But knowing where each stands gives you clarity. That's what a sexual ethic is for: making empowered, informed, authentic decisions that feel good *to you.*

From Analyst to Assassin

The work of the Analyst is *not* to carry all the things. The work of the Analyst is to notice what she is carrying. That is it. She is already physically strong enough to carry the pack. What is mentally harder is deciding what she no longer needs.

In the Tetons, I had to decide that I was okay with not taking my big DSLR camera. It was precious to me, but I had to be okay with leaving it behind because I had my iPhone camera, which was small and served my purpose. The big camera no longer served me. It just weighed me down. There was a time in my life when all I used was the big, fancy camera. But that was when the twins were small and I was at home most of the time. I wasn't out exploring the Tetons and hiking sixteen miles a day. Different time. Different environment. Different needs.

There was a time in my sexual reclamation when I had to lovingly release some of my sexual boundaries. Not allowing a partner to touch my clitoris in high school served me well because I wasn't ready. And feeling shame—like I was dirty—about a boyfriend I loved touching my genitals when I was *absolutely* ready in college no longer served me. I had to lovingly release that from my backpack and let that shame live in the past. Each day that I carried shame around genital touch was a day too long because it created distance between me and my hiking partner. But I never would have been able to remove it had I not taken time to look inside my backpack.

Notice, notice, notice.

Sometimes, we carry what is necessary—like bear repellent. Bear repellent is in a big can. We do not carry it because it is lovely or we like it. We carry it because we have to. Because it is necessary.

You carry some stuff about sex because it is necessary. You will have to shuffle the items in your bag because these things will always be there. These include traumatic events and past experiences. But you may not have to carry the messages around these events so they don't feel so heavy. You can move the bear spray can from the top of your pack, where it shifts and topples your weight from side to side and hurts your shoulders every step, to the bottom of your pack, where the weight is carried mostly on your strong hips. You hardly feel it. The weight of trauma can be moved and supported by the strongest parts of you—the parts that understand how to manage triggers, irrational thoughts, and anxiety. Sometimes, you can let somebody in your hiking group carry the bear repellent for a bit. Sometimes, you let a friend or a professional carry the weight of your past experiences when you need some support. Either way, the can must get carried.

Last, there is other stuff that never served you well and will never serve you well—not in the past, present, or future. This is like carrying cinder blocks. They are heavy messages that only slow you down and create distance between you and your partner.

Harmful cinder-block messages that I'm tired of carrying:

Nobody will want me if I have sex before I'm married.

My worth is defined by my body.

I should never turn down my husband's desire for sex.

If I don't want sex, it must mean I don't love my partner.

My genitals are dirty and shouldn't be touched.

Masturbation is wrong.

My pleasure is secondary to my partner's pleasure.

My body is what makes my partner want to have sex with me.

My partner will not want me to speak up about my needs.

Penetrative sex is the only real sex.

These cinder-block messages do nothing but harm. They weigh you down and keep you distant. They are crappy, dead-weight, good-for-nothing messages. Your Analyst has done the work of identifying these messages in the bag. Her work here is done.

My darling, your cinder blocks are waiting.

It's time to crush them.

Part 2:
The Assassin

"You may not control all the events that happen to you,
but you can decide not to be reduced by them."
— *Maya Angelou*

The Assassin doesn't ask for permission. She takes aim and fires. She is the part of you that refuses to be polite in the face of oppression—the warrior who sharpens her blade on every purity culture lie you've been force-fed.

She has one mission: destruction. Not of you but of the toxic narratives that have kept you small, ashamed, and afraid of your own body.

But she is more than just a destroyer. She is a guard. She stands at the gates of your past, protecting the younger versions of you who still whisper their fears into your adult life.

The girl who felt dirty for her arousal.

The teen who was told her worth was between her legs and that she must keep them closed at all costs.

The woman who still flinches at desire.

The Assassin shields them now. She cuts down the voices that haunt you, slices through the shame you were never meant to carry, and obliterates the idea that you must stay trapped in your pain. This is your moment to let her loose and give her the power to destroy what no longer serves you. Because before you can rebuild, you have to clear the wreckage.

Chapter 6: Tapping Into Anger

I am an easygoing, calm, and cool Enneagram Nine. Fighting does not come easy for me. However, anger does. I didn't know this until I took a good look in my backpack. Once I knew what tools I had, I could become a fighter and not just be passive-aggressive.

I've learned that anger bubbles underneath my muscles on most days. Most days, I don't acknowledge or even actively disavow its very existence. How could I, with all my serenity and order and calm, be . . . (gasp . . . whisper) angry?

It's true. Most people would never know it, but it's there. I have also learned that my anger originates from days and days of conceding and not speaking up. From many conversations in which I allowed myself to hold back and not bring myself forward. It originates from watching injustices happen to others without using my voice to stop or at least highlight them.

Before I understood how my anger got here, I felt ashamed for letting it loose, very randomly, when I couldn't take it anymore. My anger would come out all yell-y and confusing, misdirected at a child or a dog or a spouse. The ones closest to me seemed to get the best of my worst.

During the tender time in my marriage—when I was experiencing so much pain during sex—the anger within me was palpable. I was angry but didn't always know why or how to fix it. So it simmered and simmered and simmered until it eventually got so hot that it boiled over.

Now I know it was trying to tell me to speak up and get help before boiling over. But at the time, I just blamed myself for being angry and felt shame for being angry about a problem that I felt was my fault.

We grow up in a world where angry women are best reserved for characters in soap operas who plot murders against cheating husbands. Real-life women need to be cool, docile, and charming. Misogyny tells us that anger isn't a good look for women—even when it is warranted.

Now I'm learning how to prevent anger that doesn't serve me (*Speak up, Celeste*) and how to use the anger that does serve me well. Anger that does serve me helps me fight and fight well. Fighting well means embracing my inner warrior—my personal Assassin.

I love Wonder Woman. I hope you have seen the Patty Jenkins 2017 film. Watch the scene where Diana (Wonder Woman) comes to understand that an entire town of innocent people is being taken captive by the Germans during World War II. She is in an American trench with Steve Trevor, an American soldier and friend, and they are shooting across this blank landscape at the Germans in the trenches three hundred yards away. They have to invade the German side to rescue the town.

Diana is insistent that they go across the land between the trenches, face the German gunfire, and try to rescue the town.

Steve vehemently disagrees, saying that they would surely perish if they tried. "No man can cross it!" he shouts over the explosions.

But she is no man.

Wonder Woman emerges from the trench, shield up and bullets pinging off her bracelets. The Americans in the trench watch in disbelief. They cannot understand what they are witnessing. Wonder Woman continues forward toward the enemy. All German gunfire focuses on her. But she is deflecting the wave of bullets.

"She's taking the fire for us!" they yell. Then they start to emerge hesitantly behind her.

Wonder Woman gains confidence, marching faster and then running, all while blocking bullet after bullet. The crew behind her starts to gain ground on the Germans. She makes it to the other side, destroys the larger guns, and continues on to rescue the town.

She rarely uses brute force. She *just wants to save the innocent.* For love. For justice.

Is this a fictional story about fictional characters with fictional powers?

Yes, and I do not care.

Because the war you will have to face in your own mind as you battle the limiting beliefs of your religious past, the entrenched media onslaught of messages, pornography's skewed bodies and behaviors, and religion's controlling bribery is *not* fiction. But it is so unfathomable that it might as well be.

It is no-man's-land.

But *you* are no man.

I'm asking you to go into battle. Walk into the fray and open yourself up to gunfire. This is a time to fight because the people in the town are waiting—**and the people in the town are earlier versions of you.**

They desperately need you to come to their aid and say, "I see you. I hear you. I know what you have been through. I know what you were told and promised. I love you, and I'm here now to protect you."

They thought they had been forgotten. They thought they had to die there, in that awful place, screaming for help, for somebody to hear them. They have been abused and traumatized and told they were worthless.

They were told they weren't pretty enough or good enough or sexy enough. Then they were told they were too sexy and too loud and too nerdy. They were told their bodies were the property of men's lust. They were left beaten, bruised, alone, and hurting.

But this is not where the story ends. You no longer have to stay in this place. You no longer have to live this version of your life.

Go to them, take their hands, and listen to their stories. Empathize with their wounds.

Tell me about the people in your town. The earlier versions of you.

Is there a little girl there who was told not to touch herself?

Is there a young woman who got sent home from school because her shorts were too short?

Is there a lady who came across her partner's porn and felt the cobra bite of comparison?

Is there a woman who never feels aroused and feels responsible for her partner's unhappiness?

Is there a sixth grader who thought if she kissed a boy, Jesus would turn his back on her?

Is there a high schooler who was terrified that her parents would find out she liked girls?

Is there a young woman in love who had the most loving and connective sexual debut, then returned home to find a pile of guilt waiting for her, causing her to break up with her boyfriend?

Is there a girl who desperately wanted somebody to talk to her honestly about sex but never found them?

I want you to fight through no-man's-land to get to these women and girls—these versions of you who were not loved in the way you needed to be loved. Look at the group. Write a letter to each of them telling them what you see and what they went through. Or talk to them using the shame reduction script you learned earlier.[6]

Brené Brown defines true belonging: "True belonging is the spiritual practice of believing in and belonging to yourself so deeply that you can share your most authentic self with the world and find sacredness in both being a part of something and standing alone in the wilderness. True belonging doesn't require you to change who you are. It requires you to be who you are."[7]

Damn.

All those earlier versions of you were trying to belong. Trying to be their most authentic self. Exploring sexuality in a way that felt right and good. And the world told you to change who you are instead of being who you are: a sexual being.

So, to help those feelings of woundedness feel smaller and more manageable, we have to go back and tell those people in the town that they were authentic and that you see their authenticity.

Tell the girl who briefly felt great after her loving sexual debut that she is right for feeling good about it. Tell the woman who finds her partner's porn that she is right for feeling angry and that she doesn't have to compare herself because she is enough. Tell the gay college girl that she is right for feeling terrified because the rest of her family was incorrect in not accepting her as she is.

It's time to cull and protect.

Activity: Give Yourself Permission to Grieve the Past

Your warrior has begun the destruction.

Great, right?

But there is one problem. The messages that you are destroying were part of your identity. So it sometimes hurts to let them go. . . even though it was also painful to let them stay.

Giving yourself permission to grieve the loss of these messages is important because, regardless of how harmful they were, they were still part of your sexual formation.

Grieving means . . . whatever it looks like to you. You might be angry that you have to do this work of deconstructing other people's mess. However long it takes and whatever resources you need to grieve a past full of messages that no longer serve you is the perfect amount.

For so many years, I had to grieve the loss of my identity as a virgin. I'd embarrassingly felt so honorable and holier because I was holding onto my earned title of purity. It took me years to understand and let go of the idea that my virginity in no way made me worthy of love and good sex. But letting go still felt painful and sad and scary.

And that's totally understandable and okay. Validate these moments for yourself.

Activity: A Grieving Ritual

This exercise is about **grieving with compassion** because even the lies we needed to survive deserve a proper send-off.

Instructions

Write a letter to a belief, message, or identity that no longer serves you. If writing isn't your thing, you can simply meditate on these prompts.

Start with:

"Dear [Cinder-Block Message About Sex], I used to believe you because . . ."

Let yourself:

- Reflect on how it once protected or guided you.
- Acknowledge what it cost you.
- Name what you're choosing instead.
- Say goodbye.

End with something like:

"Thank you for what you tried to be. I release you now."

Take your time. Cry. Rage. Burn the letter or keep it in a sacred spot. This is your compassionate grieving ritual.

Chapter 7: My Origin Story—Parents, Community, Pastors, Church

During my sexual renovation, there came a time when I had to come face-to-face with my sexual formation and make peace with it. Writing down certain points, places, and feelings of my childhood was helpful in creating a template I could use to continue my growth. Once I wrote down the stories and experiences that shaped my idea of sex, I started to find themes. (Always the data nerd.) It gave me a platform of understanding that allowed me to give myself empathy for my own situation. But it also helped me see where those themes, like responsibility, fear, and shame, were showing up in my adult life.

Anytime you dig into your childhood, there are risks and benefits. First, there's the risk of remembering sucky stuff you probably forgot in order to cope. But you also have the benefit of possibly remembering stuff that was awesome. Regardless of the risks and benefits, it is part of what makes you, you. And when you better understand your formation, you can go forward with more clarity.

My purity/abstinence ring was silver and had a heart with a gold dove on the top. I wore it from the time I started my period until the day I got married and replaced it with a wedding band. Jewelry was not allowed at my Christian school, so I often wore it hidden on a necklace under my shirt, Frodo style, so I wouldn't get in trouble.

Read that slowly one more time so you can catch the intense irony of purity culture: I wore my *abstinence ring* on a necklace *underneath my shirt* so I wouldn't get in trouble *for wearing jewelry*.

The ring was a constant part of my life—an inevitable reminder of what I should be doing. A reminder that I was special. *Pure.* The longer I wore it, the more abstinence and purity became part of who I was. I was a virgin. That was part of my label. Tall, white, kind, silly, loud . . . and virgin.

Before I go down this rabbit hole of my conservative Christian upbringing, let me just clear the air about my actual parents.

My parents are amazing. They are both high school teachers, which says a lot about their ability to handle skylarking and buffoonery. They were and continue to be more progressive than others in their very conservative town. I was lucky. The primary influences in my household were honest and open about sex. Their openness and willingness to educate me in a comprehensive way probably did more to keep me out of trouble than my community's restrictive messages did. My parents were the grace in a restrictive, controlling culture.

I actually don't recall not knowing about sex. My mom was especially great at creating lines of communication and keeping them open and honest. She told me early on that sex is not just for making babies but also for pleasure and connection. We had the famous *Where Did I Come From?* book, and I was fascinated by the picture of all the sperm going in one direction in the front layout. The cartoon drawings and rhymes have been burned into my memory. "Vagina rhymes with North Carolina."

You're welcome.

When I asked her about masturbation, she assured me that it was normal and okay and that I shouldn't feel bad about it. This was a message that exactly zero of my friends received. Even though she (and Dad) wanted me to wait until marriage to have sex, I never felt like I would be ostracized (from them) if I didn't. When it came from them, it always felt like a suggestion for my health instead of a demand for holiness.

My mom let me choose the purity ring I wanted out of a few selections in the James Avery catalog. She gave me the ring at a special dinner and explained that it was a symbol of my purity. I was excited, mostly because I was being allowed—no, *encouraged*—to wear jewelry. (Remember, my Christian community also discouraged jewelry. Oh, the mixed messages.) And abstinence was cool too. But let's be honest—abstinence wasn't exactly a *struggle* for eighth-grade Celeste.

At the time of the special dinner and the ring selection, I was thirteen and had never kissed anyone. Nor were there any suitors on the horizon. At thirteen, I was already six feet tall and towered over most of my teachers, much less any young gentlemen in my tiny eighth-grade class of twenty-four. I did spend a lot of time thinking about kissing somebody, dreaming about the day it would happen, talking with my girlfriends about when it would happen, and ripping photos of JTT* out of *Big Bopper* magazines and placing them on my wall. I also *practiced* kissing while Bryan Adams's "Have You Ever Really Loved a Woman?"† oozed from my cassette player.

I was as sexual as one could be all by oneself, even though I'd never had an actual kiss with a living, breathing human.

But other than knowing how babies are made and that it is supposed to be fun, I still had precious little information about sex.

For example, I'd hilariously already had my purity ring for months before I understood what the term *virgin* actually means. My friend James and I were in the front of the school, waiting for our parents to pick us up, when he casually said something like "Oh, well, you know she is still a virgin" when referring to somebody in a TV show we both watched. I had heard the term *virgin* only in reference to the mother of Jesus, so I quickly asked him what he meant. He side-eyed me and raised an eyebrow, like only he could, and said, "Girl, it's when you haven't had sex!"

Oh! A thousand floating pieces of information dropped, clearly organized, into a large jigsaw puzzle. I could finally see the landscape.

The Virgin Mary had not had *sex* with Joseph! And she still got pregnant! And that is why the birth of Jesus is, like, a miracle! *Oh, man!* The vocabulary details really did matter in this case. Up until eighth grade, I'd thought the term *virgin* simply meant "holy." I had no idea it had to do with not putting a penis inside your body. This whole time, I'd thought Mary got pregnant with

---

* That is Jonathan Taylor Thomas, for any of you fetuses born after 1986.

† This song stands the test of time. It's just as hot now as it was in eighth grade. Go ahead and throw it onto your sexy playlist.

Joseph's kid and God had just blessed the kid and decided that this particular kid would be Jesus because *Mary was super holy and made good choices.*

Apparently, I was an advocate for women from the very beginning.

I want to pause here and note that at this time, I knew sex was supposed to be pleasant and fun. *Also,* I was taught that pregnancy was to be avoided at all costs, was painful, and was not pleasant or fun. I also feel rather smug that the son of God entered this world through a vulva. According to history, only a uterus and a vulva (plus divine insemination) were needed to conceive and deliver Jesus onto this planet. Nary a penis in sight. I think we need to believe it happened this way because no human man would have been willing to *not* take credit for the son of God if his penis had been used to create him.

I grew up feeling sorry for Mary, but now I understand. She was a virgin, after all. She was free. She was a woman to herself, owned by nobody. She was amazing not because of her sexual chastity but because of her sexual independence. She didn't need a partner to be fully herself.

I digress. Now let's come back to the 1990s.

In high school, my friend Kimber once noticed my ring sitting on my desk instead of on my finger or around my neck. She slyly snuck it into her pocket as she walked by. Later that day, she dangled in front of my nose, laughingly indicating that she had, in quotes, "stolen my virginity." I thought it was funny, and we forever joked that she was truly my first.

It was funny, but the irony was there. Was my virginity a *thing*? Like an item that could be easily stolen off a desk? Was my virginity an object?

Was I an object?

On a rainy Texas fall day, I sat in a folding chair in our school's music room while a brave parent told the room full of girls that our virginity was like a brownie. Once somebody takes a bite out of a brownie, it becomes less appealing. And the more bites there are, the less anyone wants the brownie. Soon, nothing is left. (Were the boys brownies too? Or were they some other dessert?)

So I was not just an object. I was an object that could *disappear*? I could become obsolete if I didn't do the *right* things? Just like that? I found my very practical self wondering, *If I wear spaghetti straps, is that a bite out of my brownie? If I wear fettuccini straps, will that help keep the boys from having uncontrollably vicious erections and therefore keep my delicious brownie self edible?*

By my senior year, I had been long-distance dating my very own first serious boyfriend for a year, and he had decided to attend college in my hometown. I was living the dream. Here I was, a high school senior with a cute, kind *college* boyfriend.

We had met at summer camp between my sophomore and junior years (his junior and senior years), and we had swiftly fallen for each other like seventeen-year-olds sometimes do. He was in Ohio, and I was in Texas that entire first year of dating, and I liked him so much that I couldn't breathe. It was glorious. I know you remember falling in love for the first time. It is all-consuming and powerful.

Luckily, I had fallen for a good one. He was kind and smart and athletic. He played soccer, which was a quirky, mysterious sport for small-town Texas. He treated me respectfully, and my parents loved him. Even my older brother, who had a tough outer shell, eventually started to like him, and they became close.

My boyfriend's respectful commitment to staying "pure" was so hot that it made it even more difficult for me to remain so. I remember one particular evening. I had met up with my boyfriend at his place, and my shirt had been, shall we say, not on my person. I knew I had to walk home, and I was running late. So I pulled my shirt back on, said goodbye, and walked out his front door just in time to see my dad pulling up in his car. My face grew hot and flushed as I realized I was very close to being in big trouble.

Dad pulled up, rolled down his window, and quipped, "Your shirt is on backward."

"No, it's not," I said. "That would be impossible." I snorted, rolled my eyes, and did *not* check my shirt. For the love of all things, I was not about to look down at it. I was hoping beyond all hopes that I was correct.

"Want a ride home?" he asked as his face softened into a smile.

For months after this, I felt *terrible*. But here's what was weird: I didn't feel awful about exploring sexuality with my boyfriend. I loved him. And he was kind and thoughtful. We were careful, slow, and ultimately still technically nonpenetrative virgins. And making out felt amazing, pleasurable, and connective. No, I didn't feel bad about that.

But I did feel awful about *disappointing my dad*.

I ruminated on this weird phenomenon for a long time. How could something that felt so good and right and safe be so bad that I could break my dad's trust in me? I was not that kind of a kid. I played by the rules. I respected my parents, and they respected me. And yet, this was the one area where I felt like I should have been allowed more privileges. More room to explore what was good for me. I truly didn't think of myself as a brownie or a ring. I was a person—a person who was learning and making healthy choices in that process. I wasn't being careless, unsafe, or hurtful to myself or others. I was exploring in a way that made sense to me in a natural progression for a relationship.

Looking back, I realize that I remained a "virgin" only because it was expected of me. Following the rules and keeping the peace were my only motivations. I figured I could engage in quite a bit of sexual activity that felt really good *and* keep my technical virginity intact. I could make both worlds happy. So I did.

So much of the abstinence talk was just . . . unhinged. I thought it was weird back then, and now it reads like badly translated Tolkien fanfic. We were told that if you had sex, you'd become *soul-tied* to that person forever. Like the moment a penis enters a vagina, it forges an unbreakable mystical bond—some Frodo-ring situation where your soul is now bound to Chad from youth group because you thought it was rad that he had a Honda Civic and a surprisingly aggressive playlist of Christian ska.

Apparently, the penis is less an organ and more of a sacred artifact—like the One Ring, forged in the fires of Mount Doom, cursed with the power to connect you to bad decisions for eternity.

And if you dare to have sex with someone else? The soul-tie spell doesn't break. Oh no. Now you're just carrying multiple enchanted burdens like a spiritual horcrux collector.

Whoever came up with the idea that the penis is a wizard staff of eternal soul fusion... definitely had one, and definitely wanted it to sound more magical than it actually was.

Other confusing statements I heard:

- "The way you dress is a stumbling block for boys." (Wait, I thought I was a brownie. I'd much rather be a brownie than a *block*.)
- "If you have sex before marriage, it is like giving your future husband a rose with no petals."
- "The only man you need in your life is Jesus until he brings you a man of the flesh."
- "Open books, not legs. Blow minds, not guys." (I do appreciate the clever marketing here.)
- "When you dress a certain way, you are committing pornography in your own life."
- "Wait for respect. Don't settle for lust." (I'll take both, please and thank you.)

I didn't honestly think that incredibly awful things were going to happen to me if I had sex. Maybe just slightly awful things. And for me, "slightly awful" would mean people would be disappointed in me. I always, always aimed to please.

My parents were more sex-positive. So, at home, I was getting the message that sex is great . . . and would be even easier and better if I waited until I was married. Mom and Dad always err on the side of love. Always. They prioritize love over everything, and it showed in how they raised my brother and me. From early on, my parents pushed back against religious rules that they thought weren't made in the direction of love. They were and are this unique combination of always faithful with a high sense of love and justice. They prioritized us and all humans, constantly reminding us that life is messy and we weren't created for perfection. We were created for relationships.

There were, however, some silver linings in not having penetrative sex. I was experienced at getting aroused and reaching orgasm by myself or with a partner. With clothes on, with clothes off, with some on and some off. If dry sex had been a degree, I would have graduated as valedictorian . . . with a minor in grinding. Since penetration with a penis remained a boundary my boyfriend and I were willing to keep, everything else became important— sensations, pleasure, talking, learning, and exploring. This was so, so good.

I now know that all of this exploration and outercourse were essential to my healing from vaginismus and the pain I experienced when I first started having penetrative sex once married. In those early days of marriage, the knowledge and experience I'd gained from so much nonpenetrative play helped me stay connected with my body and with Nate and get back to associating sexual touch with pleasure instead of pain. But in high school, the only thing I felt about these experiences was *guilt*.

I still felt so, so guilty.

This is just a small part of my upbringing, but you can already see patterns and themes emerge. Here are some themes I have mined from these stories.

- Responsibility
- Shame
- Guilt
- Neglect (As in I didn't get enough information to be able to make choices that were right for me)

Activity: Sexual Messaging

Take some time to write down your sexual origin story using the prompts below. Find the messages and themes you received growing up and start by answering these prompts. Once you have answered the questions, reread your words and look for themes. I've given you a common list of themes you can choose from. Or you can find your own.

- Who told you about sex, and how old were you? What was the general message?
- Did you have a trusted adult you could talk to about sex?
- Did you masturbate growing up? If so, were you shamed for doing it? Or did you get caught or punished?
- Were your clothes policed when you were growing up?
- Were you told you were responsible for the boy's behavior?
- What did you feel emotionally when you first started to sexually explore?
- Are there more traumatic experiences that created a thought pattern around sex?
- Did you go to church growing up? What was the message about sex there?
- Did you attend public or private school? Did you have sex education at school?
- Were you exposed to explicit material growing up? How did you feel about this material?

Here is a list of common themes and emotions that come up with these messages:

- Neglect
- Responsibility
- Fear
- Shame
- Guilt
- Danger

You may have your own list. These are just some that come up frequently with my clients.

Find the messages, then find the themes. In the next section, we will work to destroy any messages that were harmful. We'll also work to heal the themes and emotions that arise from those messages. Remember you might want to do this with the help of a therapist or mental health provider, considering it might bring up memories of trauma.

Chapter 8: Shame, Fear, and Trauma

From the view of my practice, there are two predictors of sexual dysfunction. Let's start with what they are not.

Sexual dysfunction is not predicted by the date you started having sex.

Or the person you began having sex with.

Or the lack of a marriage certificate.

Or the sexual positions or behaviors.

It is shame. Shame is the biggest predictor of sexual dysfunction, followed closely by lack of education.[8]

The enormous power of a woman and the negative power of culture can create a deadly combination: shame. I see this every day: women and couples feeling broken and unworthy, comparing their relationships and sex lives to others, being confused, and making risky choices.

There are three core focus areas I see most often in my practice: painful intercourse, low libido, and sexual shame. I create safe spaces where people can talk about sex so they can work through these issues.

At this point, I have been in the business long enough to be able to easily identify shame, especially when it surfaces in sexual experiences or beliefs. Shame is the first layer of dysfunction that leads to more concrete challenges like low libido or pain. However, when we don't have common conversations about shame (how shameful!), it is sometimes hard to identify or recognize when it shows up.

Let's have a conversation about what shame is and how it may be showing up in your life.

Shame, by definition in Merriam-Webster, is "a painful feeling of humiliation or distress caused by the consciousness of wrong or foolish behavior."[9]

Let's dissect this from the beginning. The first term in the definition of shame is "painful feeling." Doesn't that just punch you in the gut? *A painful feeling.*

Then the words *humiliation* and *distress*. Wow.

Painful, humiliating, distressing.

Sounds a bit like *trauma*, doesn't it?

The rest of the definition is as you would expect. "Caused by the consciousness of wrong or foolish behavior." If I could write to the Definition People, I would politely request to add the word *perceived* before *consciousness*. The definition would then read like this:

"Shame: A painful feeling of humiliation or distress caused by the *perceived* consciousness of wrong or foolish behavior."

The perception of what is wrong or foolish in sex is very subjective. What may feel wrong for you might feel right for me. Or what might feel wrong for you at twenty-three might feel very right for you at forty-three. Unfortunately, shame could care less about perception. The pain and distress caused by shame continue to harm individuals *even* when their *perception* of what is "wrong" or "foolish" has altered.

Why?

Because shame is powerful, lasting, and irrational. It isn't there to help you do better or feel better. Its goal is to keep you in a heightened state of alarm. It's nasty, insidious, and circular. That's what makes it powerful.

Shame happens when we have no other skills for coping. It is a defense mechanism, but it is built on perceptions, which we have identified can be wrong or misplaced. So, shame walks in when we don't have any other skills. But I hope you are learning the skills to address shame in sex so it is no longer with you.

Sometimes, we lump shame in with guilt. In my opinion, shame and guilt are very different. Guilt is a defense mechanism that helps us cope and gives us the impetus to course correct. If we never felt guilt, we might be pretty terrible people. Or at least I think I would. Guilt is provided by consciousness, that little angel on your shoulder or whatever you want to call the inner workings of your being that gives you a twinge of second-guessing when you are about to yell at your dog for something that was your fault. It is there to keep you and others safe. Guilt also helps push you toward learning and vulnerability so you can do things better the next time. When guilt works well, it can help you.

But a clear distinction between guilt and shame is this: Guilt is about your *behaviors* and passes quickly once the course has been corrected. For example, if you feel better after apologizing and making things right, the guilt feeling was helpful and can now pass through. Shame is about your being and who you are in your core, *not* your behaviors. Guilt says, "I made a mistake." Shame says, "I *am* a mistake."[10] Shame settles deep and tells you that you aren't enough. You will never be enough.

I love this description in *Tattoos on the Heart:*

> Guilt, of course, is feeling bad about one's actions, but shame is feeling bad about oneself. Failure, embarrassment, weakness, overwhelming worthlessness, and feeling 'less than'—all permeating the marrow of the soul.[11]

Shame is the message that you are wrong at your core. Industries like the beauty industry and, specifically, the diet industry capitalize on the power of shame.

Activity: Shame Reduction Script

What do you do with traumatic shame?

In the next section, we will do some cognitive work around reducing the impact of fear messaging. But for now, I want to give you a tool you can use immediately when you might feel triggered.

The Shame Resilience Theory by Brené Brown[12] can help us combat the symptoms of shame when they arise. This may feel like anxiety (heaviness in the chest and heart racing) or depression (heaviness in the mind and dullness of sensory experience). Are you feeling any of these in this moment? Or do you feel any of these when you think about when you're having to have sex or just after sex?

My therapist taught me to use a shame reduction script, which is based on the work of Thich Nhat Hanh, to help me find compassion for myself in moments when I felt shame. It's the idea of separating your current self from your earlier versions of you—the ones who were acutely feeling the infliction of these messages. Picture an earlier version of you sitting in the room with you. She might be twelve-year-old you, twenty-three-year-old you, or a version of you from two weeks ago. Speak to her like you would to your best friend, being compassionate and kind.

My therapist taught me to put my hand on my heart and speak kindly to my "committee"—those earlier versions of myself. These are the words I say to myself.

Re-Parenting Script for Sexual Shame

By Celeste Holbrook, PhD

Younger (your name) within me,

I feel your sexual shame, confusion, or fear.

There is nothing wrong with your desires or your body. There never has been.

I remember what you went through—how you felt guilty, judged, or unsafe.

I'm so sorry no one protected you. I'm sorry no one gave you enough information about sex to help you make decisions that were perfect for you.

I am here for you now, and I will protect you.

You don't have to continue to show up and warn me of these feelings in my current sex life.

That's my job. You are safe here in my heart, where you belong.

I will take care of life.

I will not leave you.

I love you.

Think about situations in which you may have felt ashamed. Think about the person you were when this experience happened and invite her to sit across from you. Either recite the re-parenting script or write her a letter in your journal, affirming her, loving her, and hearing how she was doing her best. Then invite her to stay in your heart, where she belongs, while you take care of your current life.

Consistent use of a re-parenting script like this one will slowly start to help your earlier you feel seen, loved, and safe. Then, the shame you feel around sexual experiences will begin to soften as well. I know it sounds woo-woo to some of you, and I thought that at first too. But it truly did work for me, and I hope it eases you into healing as well.

Flight, Fight or Freeze

Purity culture and exploitative sex culture messages create shame by springboarding off fear. Fear is an incredibly effective motivator for behavior change, but it can have devastating effects on your body when used in inappropriate scenarios. A fear response is meant to keep you safe from things like being attacked by a bear, not from the size and shape of your body. Here is how fear works in *appropriate* scenarios to keep you safe.

Let's pretend you are out having a lovely walkabout in the Australian Outback when a rabid kangaroo jumps out of the brush and heads your way to attack. Your brain immediately analyzes the situation to make a plan, focusing first on the threat.

In less than a second, Brain says, "Rabid kangaroo, six feet tall, speeding toward me. What do I know about kangaroos? They are fast, typically adorable marsupials that lean back on their tail and kick when threatened. They have glutes for days. Kicks from an adorable marsupial will probably hurt me."

In this moment, Brain must decide on an appropriate course of action: *Flee, fight,* or *freeze.*

"Kangaroo is larger than me," Brain decides. "It will kick me if feeling threatened, which looks probable at this point. Kangaroo looks like it goes hard on leg day at the gym, so *fighting* is not in my favor. Kangaroo is staring me down like I stare at the desserts in a slow potluck line. So *freezing* and hoping he doesn't notice me also doesn't seem like the best road to survival. The last option is to try and outrun the kangaroo and get to a safe place. Body, I choose *flee.* Final answer."

Body replies, "Let's do this!"

In preparation for fleeing, the body shuts down any nonessential systems. According to the super-smart neuroscientists,[13] when the brain decides to fight, freeze, or flee, it signals the body to dilate the pupils for better eyesight, dilate the bronchi for better breathing, and increase the heart rate for faster blood flow to needed muscles.

Organs and systems that are not vital in the moment will shut down. This may include your gastrointestinal tract . . . which is why you may poop your pants when you get super-duper scared. It's science.

This last bit about nonessential systems shutting down is very important. Remember this.

Now, back to the rabid kangaroo. Body does the work of amping up the helpful systems (blood flow to leg muscles) and turning off the unhelpful systems (digestion). This happens in less than a blink of an eye.[14] You flee up a nearby eucalyptus tree, where you sit until the kangaroo passes. You are safe and no worse for wear, except that you pooped your pants.

However, on your next walkabout, you walk around a bush and see another kangaroo. It's not a rabid one—just a regular, non-threatening, adorable marsupial. At first, Brain is on high alert and says, *Flee!* After a few seconds, Brain cognitively overrides the thought that the kangaroo is a threat, but it's too late. Body has already kicked into gear.

Body says, *"Let's do this!"*

And you poop your pants.

How does this apply to sex messages?

When sex messages instill a sense of fear, your brain must digest the fear message and send a directive to your body.

Let's say you're fourteen, sitting in a True Love Waits conference, and being told that you will go to hell if you have sex before you are married. No problem. You are a six-foot-tall tomboy who loves horses and reading. Nobody seems to register you as sexual anyway, so avoiding sex shouldn't be an issue.

In less than a second, Brain says, "Sex will send me to hell. Hell seems hot and full of disgruntled individuals. We don't want to go there. So . . . sex is harmful *but* not chasing me in this moment. So there is no reason to flee. Sex also doesn't seem to want to fight me either. So fighting seems to exert too much energy for Body. Freeze? Yes, freeze seems the appropriate response for sex. I will take this information and log it for future use."

Body says, *"Let's freeze!"*

Fast-forward twelve years. Over those twelve years, Brain told Body to freeze during any sexual stimuli. Now, on the wedding night, the sexual stimuli are there, and Body responds to Brain's conditioning.

Brain says on wedding night, "Ah, remember that sex is harmful and will send you to the hot place with the terrible humans. Freeze the systems!"

Body says, *"Let's freeze!"*

And all the systems not needed in that moment get frozen— including the sexual response systems. The vagina doesn't make room for penetration. The tissues do not produce vaginal lubrication. The skin even negatively reacts to touch.

But Cognitive Brain (this is Brain's twin, who is separating response systems from thinking) is trying to override Body because Cognitive Brain remembers signing a marriage contract, walking down the aisle, and saying, "I do." So, Cognitive Brain is desperately trying to signal "safety" to Body so it can consciously move forward with sex. But Body is hardwired to respond to sexual stimuli by freezing. Body is shutting down the arousal systems even though Cognitive Brain continues to override and try to move forward with sexual behavior.

Vaginal penetration happens despite Body's freezing of the sexual arousal system.

Sex is full of pain.

Body is actively trying to keep itself safe from the perceived harm of going to hell, even though that isn't a real threat anymore (and never was). Body is trying its best! But Brain is also trying its best.

Unfortunately, they now have dueling messages—one that is desperately new and one that has been hardwired for twelve years. And the hardwired message is now confirmed.

Body says, "See? Sex was painful. I was right. We should have frozen all the way. You suck, Brain. Now I have to deal with this pain. Don't ever do that again. And if you try, we will shut down harder."

Sometimes, that means pain. Sometimes, that means low libido. Sometimes, that means sexual shutdown. Most of the time, these experiences inevitably lead to shame.

Our bodies are just doing their job, trying to protect us from the danger that we were told sex was. So we end up feeling wrong when we can't perform in the way we are told we are supposed to perform.

We think, *I'm not good enough. My body isn't good enough. My genitals aren't good enough. My sexual offerings aren't good enough.*

And presto, we have a Body vs. Brain battle over sex that wreaks havoc on relationships and sex lives.

Fear Instills Trauma

(Trigger Warning: Sexual Abuse Mentioned)

The American Psychological Association has this to say about sexual abuse.

> Sexual abuse is unwanted sexual activity with perpetrators using force, making threats or taking advantage of victims not able to give consent. Most victims and perpetrators know each other. Immediate reactions to sexual abuse include shock, fear or disbelief. Long-term symptoms include anxiety, fear or post-traumatic stress disorder. While efforts to treat sex offenders remain unpromising, psychological interventions for survivors — especially group therapy — appears effective.[15]

How does this relate to us closing off on our wedding nights? Stay with me. I'd like to take a pass at rewriting this paragraph. Let's see if we can find anything revealing about *purity culture* in a paragraph that defines sexual abuse. My additions to make this relevant are added in italics:

> Sexual abuse is unwanted sexual activity, *including harmful sexual communication,* with perpetrators using force; making threats, *like you will be unloved or go*

to hell; or taking advantage of victims unable to give
consent, *like underage people being forced to sit in a True
Love Waits conference.* Immediate reactions to this kind
of abuse include shock, fear, or disbelief. Most victims
and perpetrators know each other. Long-term symptoms
include anxiety, fear, or post-traumatic stress disorder.
While efforts to treat sex offenders, *like religious leaders
who push abstinence **only** agendas,* remain unpromising,
psychological interventions for survivors—especially
group work, *like a bunch of women coming forward to col-
lectively support each other regarding their sexual upbringing*—appears effective.

Trauma, as the Somatic Institute describes, can stem from "too
much, too soon, too fast"—flooding the nervous system—or from
"not enough, too late, too little,"[16] leaving deep scars of neglect.
When it comes to purity culture and the lack of comprehensive
sexual education, many of us experience the latter: Critical information about our bodies, boundaries, pleasure, and consent was
withheld or delivered too late to build a foundation of safety and
trust within ourselves. This absence isn't neutral—it creates a
kind of hollow trauma, where confusion, shame, and disconnection quietly take root, not because of what was done, but because
of what was *missing* when we needed it most.

The sexual communication and education (or lack of) many of us
received growing up incited fear and induced neglectful trauma.
Period. The more I do this work, the more convinced I am that
purity culture messages, no matter how rooted in "love" they were
intended to be, are traumatic. The more women I see in my practice who are experiencing anxiety, fear, or post-traumatic stress
disorder surrounding sex without other types of sexual abuse
present in their history, the more sure I am that these harmful
messages induce trauma.

Activity: Purity Culture and Exploitative Sex Culture Messages Are Rooted in Fear

Here are examples of the messages that both purity culture and exploitative sex culture generate. I want you to match the type of fear to the messages.

Type of Fear

Fear of sickness _____

_____

_____

Fear of loneliness _____

_____

_____

Fear of going to hell _____

_____

_____

Fear of not belonging _____

_____

_____

Fear of missing out _____

_____

_____

Purity Culture Messages

- "If you touch your genitals, you are dirty and a sinner."
- "If you have sex before you are married, nobody will want to marry you. You will be unlovable."

- "If you have sex, you are going to get an STI or become pregnant."
- "If you like sex too much, you won't look like a Christian."
- "If you watch porn, your mind will be broken forever."
- "If you do this sex thing with the wrong person or at the wrong time, you will go to hell."

Exploitative Sex Messages

- "If you don't have sex, nobody will want to stay with you."
- "If you don't look this certain way, nobody will think you are attractive enough for sex."
- "If you wait so long to have sex, you will regret missing those experiences."
- "If you are a virgin when you get married, you won't know if you are compatible with your mate."
- "If you don't love sex, something is wrong with you."

The fear says you won't be or aren't enough. This message lives within you and becomes shame. This entire process is trauma.

Challenge and Reframe Sex Messages

Look at your cinder-block messages. Read through every single one. Do you find a theme? I bet I can guess what that theme is: fear. Most of the messages doled out by purity culture and exploitative sex culture are fear-based.

Chapter 9: Body Image—A Harm-Reduction Approach

You can't write a book about sex and not include a chapter on body image.

I've heard countless women admit that they are self-conscious about how their body looks during sex. The thought "Am I good enough?" will supersede your ability to get aroused a majority of the time. Negative thoughts about your body keep you from the liberation of letting go during sex. These thoughts hold you back and keep your pleasure small.

In this chapter, I hope to shine some light not just on how we rein in those negative thoughts but also on why we have them in the first place. The more we can push the responsibility of negative body thoughts back to the true originators—the beauty industry and the patriarchy—the easier it will feel to accept your body as it is.

Accepting your body as it is just might be one of the wildest, most courageous steps you can take to make your sex life real and your real life exceptional.

Good or Pretty

My friend's grandaddy had an expression he would say as we scrambled out the door for a night out: "If you can't be good, be pretty!"

I think about this often. Be good or be pretty. Good *or* pretty. Either or. But not both and. Never both.

Despite what people say, it is still difficult for our culture to reconcile that a girl can be both good *and* pretty. It just feels so weird. And if a girl could be both, she would need to be pretty first in order for us to pay enough attention to see that she is also good. Pretty is the price we pay to have an audience notice that we are also competent, kind, and resilient.

Legally Blonde's plot and our interest in Reese Witherspoon's character, Elle, completely depends on this being true. We are pulled into the plot because it's rare to witness a female lead being smart, good, and conventionally pretty or sexy.

"*Legally Blonde* questioned women's place as primarily sexual creatures, allowing a stereotypically 'feminine' and attractive woman to flaunt her girlishness while also kicking ass in court."[17] We see an updated version of this in our beloved *Barbie* movie from 2023.

Our culture loves dichotomy. Patriarchy continues to push the idea of beauty in a thin lane (pun intended) as the only path to success and fulfillment. Look at our advertising. Although the tide is shifting, if you open any retail clothing website, you will see *mostly* images of straight-size, hairless models with flawless, photoshopped skin that tempt you to believe that these clothes will make you prettier.

Again, patriarchal culture says pretty is the price you must pay to get an audience.

Our culture still values the female body over the female brain. Culture insists we must try to be beautiful first. The trillion-dollar beauty industry is fueled by the concept of desire. Desire is the longing for something you don't have. As long as you desire to look different, you are controllable from a marketing perspective. And how does that industry get you to desire to look different?

Simple. It tells you that you are wrong. Specifically, that you *look* wrong. And the culture has been telling many people that they have been wrong from the day they were born.

"Beauty" is our admission fee to a "good life." But I'm broke and tired of binge-watching this show.

You are enough.

When are we going to step off this treadmill and stop running after somebody else's lame, destructive, and unattainable version of beautiful or good?

The answer?

When you accept that you are enough.

Too much hair, not enough hair, too much fat, not enough fat, too outspoken, too shy, too dry, too oily, too bushy, too smart for your own good, too flat, too tall, too short . . . Wrong, wrong, wrong. As long as you feel wrong, you will have a desire to fix it.

And a desire to feel right. As soon as you change all this, you'll feel right, right?

Wrong.

You will feel right when you accept that you were born right. Period.

After I gave birth to the twins—and had gained a significant amount of weight—I felt a lot of pressure to "bounce back"—to get my physical appearance looking like I had never gained weight while growing two persons inside my body cavity. So I tried to eat "right" (whatever the fuck that means) and move my body in ways that would burn lots of calories. (Calorie deficit! That's all you need to be the queen of beauty—fewer calories.)

And I did all this while trying to keep two humans alive by giving them more calories from my boobs. Calories! They needed the calories to survive because they needed to grow and get big! But those calories, apparently, needed to come from only my boobs, not from formula. I was expected to provide boob-only calories to make the twins bigger. But I felt the pressure to not consume too many calories myself because then *I* would be bigger. "Don't be bigger," our culture says, "except in your boobs. It's great to be bigger in your boobs. Well, unless they are so big that they sag. Or so big that they distract unwoke men from doing their great work of existing. Then your boobs need to be smaller. But not so small that they can't feed the two humans. Definitely feed the humans with your medium-size, perky, not saggy boobs. But not in public, please. That's so gross."

If you have ever wanted to change a part of your body, join the club. There are billions of us with this particularly painful subscription service. But I don't want you to feel bad about wanting to change your body. This isn't your fault. The beauty culture is the one dragging you to the altar of *desire to change*. You are not to blame. As long as you feel unwelcome in the body you have, the beauty industry, which is built on patriarchy, thrives.

In *The Beauty Myth*,[18] Naomi Wolf says, "A woman who hates her body is a tractable one." Basically, a woman who hates her body is a *controllable* one. Diet culture and beauty culture want you to continue to desire change because that is the only way they can continue to exist. If you continue to desire to look different, they can continue to sell you stuff you think you need.

As a practitioner whose purpose is to help women feel worthy, I had to find a way to survive in a culture that says I need to change *and* find ways to tear down those very constructs.

Harm-Reduction Approach to Negative Body Thoughts

Black women have been leading the way on the topic of body liberation for centuries, and it is important to note that we wouldn't have Eurocentric standards of beauty without white supremacy. So it makes sense that Black women have had to deal with this bullshit the longest and have had to resist the hardest.

In the 1960s, amid the civil rights and feminist movements, Black women confronted the compounded biases of racism and fatphobia. They were often subjected to derogatory stereotypes in the media. This misrepresentation spurred the emergence of fat activism, which focused on dismantling the intertwined prejudices of misogyny and racism and promoting body acceptance for marginalized communities, including people of color and LGBTQ+ individuals.[19]

The formation of the Grandassa Models in 1962 marked a significant milestone in the body liberation movement. Founded by Kwame Brathwaite and Elombe Brath, this group was central to the Black Is Beautiful movement, which emphasized natural Black beauty and challenged Eurocentric beauty standards. The Grandassa Models celebrated a range of body sizes and skin tones, wearing their hair naturally at a time when such expressions were considered unconventional. Their annual Miss Natural Standard of Beauty contests in Harlem became a platform for redefining beauty norms and empowering Black women to embrace their authentic selves.[20]

The introduction of whiteness into Black women's body liberation created a space more dominated by white, cisgender, and smaller-body individuals, which often sidelined the lived experiences and voices of those facing intersecting oppressions. The whitewashed message of body positivity is a weaker version, one that largely ignores gender identity. The more generalized and commercialized message of self-love and acceptance frequently neglected the systemic issues of racism and fatphobia that disproportionality affect Black women.[21]

To honor the roots and effect meaningful change, we must continue to center the experiences of Black women (especially Black queer women), ensuring that we continue to dismantle the societal structures that perpetuate the marginalization of bodies.

But what about when I'm at home, looking in the mirror? Even though I'm a straight-sized, able-bodied white lady, I *still* want to change my body. Why is that? And what do I *actually* do about that?

Shift the focus. You and your body are not the problem. Our culture and society are the problem.

This shift makes sense to me and ultimately has helped me with some areas of my body I continue to have negative thoughts about.

Ultimately, the beauty culture standard is what needs to change, not me. However, the process of fighting against those ideals still falls within the circle of women.

Brands like Fenty Beauty, Jibri, and ThirdLove are painting a new picture of what beauty can look like in front of the camera. They are inviting the cellulite and the blotchy skin and the fat rolls into the light so we can begin to see ourselves as beautiful too. Social media influencers are starting to do the same. It takes everyone pushing the wall from different perspectives to tear it down.

As much work as I do to generally feel good moving about the world in my personal skin sack, I still employ behaviors that make me more *agreeable* to beauty culture. I sometimes wear makeup. I cover up my dark spots and my zits. I have multiple pairs of Spanx. I often wear eyelash extensions. I employ hair removal techniques and own a few padded bras. Sometimes, these tactics make me believe I feel good—even sexy. Other times, these "beauty" routines make me feel sad, like I am losing my own internal battle with negative feelings about my body. However, I have concluded that when I'm wearing these masks, I think less about what other people (society) are thinking about my body. It's not conforming to standards. It's putting on armor.

I'm reducing the harm I experience.

When I began the work of freeing my body from these standards, I felt like a fraud. How could I advocate for women to embrace and accept exactly who they are while wearing a push-up bra? How could I be an intersectional feminist fighting for women's rights while also participating in the system meant to keep us too occupied to see our own suffering?

Almost suddenly one day, it occurred to me: I don't have to feel bad about wearing eyelash extensions while fighting for body acceptance. Because the work of changing beauty standards shouldn't be my responsibility. It should be the responsibility of those who *create* the unrealistic standards. We didn't create this phenomenon. Therefore, we are not responsible for fixing it. We are responsible only for educating ourselves enough to know the difference.

It occurred to me that I can go all in and fight patriarchy in heels or tennis shoes, jeans or cocktail dress, no bra, padded bra, bikini, stretch marks showing, belly out, FUPA, and eyelash extensions. It didn't matter. What mattered was that I felt safe enough to fight.

Feeling empowered means taking control over feeling safe by using strategies that protect you from a world that's fixated on the narrow, Eurocentric ideal of beauty and imposes shame upon you if you don't fit in. Whether it's choosing a padded bra, following a precise makeup routine, or opting for a power suit with high heels and statement accessories, these tactics aren't about hiding who you are. They're about reclaiming your autonomy.

Here, *imposed shame* refers to the guilt and embarrassment that society forces upon you when you don't conform to its unrealistic standards—a cultural burden that makes you feel inherently flawed. By selecting what makes you feel confident, you reduce the harm that these external judgments inflict. It might not bring unbridled joy, but it minimizes the distraction of self-doubt so you can keep fighting for your true self.

Sara Landry, one of my favorite Instagram follows—@thebirdspapaya—has a beautiful reframe for how to talk to yourself about your coping strategies:

- Instead of "My hair looks good, so I feel good," say, "I'm so glad I spent some extra time on me today. That feels good."

- Instead of "Red lipstick makes me feel fierce," try "I feel fierce, and wearing something bold really reflects it."

When I cope in certain standard-beauty-conforming ways, I show up better for those I serve. I can give a stronger, more poignant presentation on helping women embrace their sexuality, vulvas, pleasure, and arousal. These women go home and strike up better, more educated conversations with their lovers and friends about sex. Finding their own pleasure from their vulvas empowers them to seek more pleasure in life. When they embrace pleasure more fully, they ask for what they need, inside and outside the bedroom. Getting their needs met helps them laugh more heartily with their partners, find softness with their children, grow more confident in their own bodies, run for office, ask for promotions, run companies, and burst through glass ceilings.

And that is the story of how wearing my fake eyelashes helps women smash the patriarchy.

Reflective Activity

Go back and reread your origin story. What messages about your body did you receive growing up? How do they influence you today? How have your messages changed? What harm-reduction strategies do you employ to help you focus?

Moving Forward
in the Battle

You use worthiness to fuel your Assassin. Here is the hard part
of the warrior: The people around you are not going to like it,
and that is why she is bloody and strong. The people around you
may feel uncomfortable with you pushing and slashing the old,
worn-out messaging. Many times, these people are the ones who
raised us.

But keep fighting for your own version of sexuality. Don't accept
messages that don't serve you.

The Assassin is our fighter for truth. She asks us how we got here:
duty, obligation, culture, or messaging? (How many times do I
hear women say, "wifely duties"?) The Assassin fights through
these mixed messages and dualities, then helps us uncover our

truth. Through this missionary, you can find what messages were given to you and how they no longer serve you. You can fight the limited messages that come from purity and patriarchy to uncover authentic truth.

What messages do you get now?

You are not fixed yet. But you do know that you are worth the journey. You might emerge bloody and hurt, but you won't ever be broken. Not even close.

Now's the time to heal.

Part 3:
The Healer

The battlefield always leaves wounds. If you aren't left hurting, you may not have flung yourself deep enough into the fray. You have just been through deconstruction, tearing away much of the "truth" that once lived deep in your sinewy fibers. When messages run that deep, the only way out is through dissection, deep wounds, and lots of slow, determined recovery.

This is where we meet the Healer within you.

As you have now been through the process of noticing and then deconstructing sexual messages that do not serve you, it is time to tend to your wound and learn how to walk again. It's time to access your own Healer. She is going to validate your pain and help you move forward by encouraging a gentle reeducation.

Your Healer validates first. Then she heals. She helps you peek out of your bunker and start something new. She is an agent of compassion and movement. Of change. Here are the lessons she brings regarding your sexual becoming.

Sex is something you learn.

Your inner Healer is your inner sex educator. Once you have uncovered and debunked unhelpful messages, you may feel a bit like, "What now? I know what is undone. But what do I do about it?"

Embrace that sex is a skill.

It's like driving a car, learning to play chess, or parenting. Sex is a skill set.

This is *good*. Most of us get the message that sex is natural and biological. While yes, sex is something we are created to do, the act of sex with self and others is something we must learn. When someone is told that sex is natural and then struggles with it, they can feel like something is deeply wrong with how they were created. This causes trauma and trouble in sex lives and relationships.

There are very few other things in life that we think we should just know. For example, we give ourselves room to learn about relationships, health, and money. Why not sex too?

Just because you are born sexual doesn't mean you know how to have good sex. Or pleasurable sex. That's something you learn— and continue to learn as you continue to experience and grow. The end of your learning is the end of your life. (And I'm not even really sure about that.)

I'm still learning too. I'm writing this book knowing that I will pick it up in a couple of years and feel differently about some parts. I sincerely hope I feel differently about sex in a couple of years because that will show that I'm listening to my inner Healer—the one who compassionately pushes me into vulnerability and growth.

The only way I *won't* feel differently about this book in a few years is if I choke on the waffle I'm eating right now and the next thing you read is my obituary. Which, by the way, I hope simply reads, "She choked to death on a waffle (her favorite breakfast) while helping people with their sex lives. Legend."

So, embrace that you will continue to learn about sex and continue to change the way you *do* sex. The couples that are most unhappy in their sex lives do not make learning about sex a priority.

Next up? A gentle reeducation.

Chapter 10: Rethinking Sex as a Goal

There are no trophies. No medals or certificates. There are no levels to be unlocked. Nobody is declared a winner, and there certainly aren't monetary prizes. (Okay, maybe sometimes? But that is not this book.)

Sex is not an achievement. Sex is an experience.

This trips a lot of people up. We get really focused on getting to the end. We even make analogies that have to do with achieving something.

"She scored."

"He went to third base."

"We finished together."

We tend to think that a sexual experience is good only if a goal is reached. Particularly orgasm.

"Did you come?"

We do this with good intentions because coming feels good. It does. We want to feel good, and we want our partner to feel good. But you already know what I'm going to say.

Sex isn't a goal.

Imagine if we always thought of food in this way.

"How was your dinner?"

"Oh, we both finished all our food. It was great!"

"But what was your dinner like? Was it delicious?"

"Oh, absolutely. We both ate everything that was offered. And at the end of the meal, we licked our plates."

"You finished the food because it was good food?"

"Oh yes, we finished the food!"

"Oh my gosh! Just tell me how the food tasted!"

"We finished it. At the same time."

We deeply understand that food is an experience, not an achievement. Unless you are a competitive hot dog eater, there are no trophies for food achievement.

Food is nourishing, salty, chewy, or hot. Fruit is wildly colorful. The fragrance of fajitas on the way to your table is the arousal phase of eating. Gelato feels smooth on the lips. Imagine the crisp snap of a perfect Frito, covered with seven-layer dip, between your teeth. The energy you feel in your cells when your coffee begins is life's calling.

Food is an experience.

Are you salivating yet?

If we can experience this level of sensuality with food, surely we can do it with sex, right?

If we want to make sex more of an experience and less of an achievement, we must redefine what sex is for us.

How would you define sex? Here are some examples of how others might define it:

- Clitoral stimulation
- Vulvas rubbing together
- Anal play with fingers
- Sexy chatting on FaceTime
- Snuggling together naked
- Watching your partner masturbate
- Penis in vagina
- Placing a dildo in your partner's anus
- Grinding a vulva against a partner's chest
- Ejaculating on skin
- Oral play
- Sexual stimulation that doesn't end in orgasm
- Dressing up in character and talking about sexual fantasies
- Being tied up and massaged

How do you define sex? When you start broadening the idea of what sex is, you can start experiencing sex instead of achieving it. The work of your Healer is to help you make sex more inclusive. The Healer's work is to include all kinds of things within the framework of sex. This is a compassionate way to look at sex because it is *inclusive*.

When the definition of sex includes experiential words like *connection* and *intimacy*, you expand your ability to experience sex, even when you are sitting together on the couch—or even when one of you is deployed or when one of you has Alzheimer's and can't consent to touch anymore.

Go back to the list where you wrote down how you felt about sex currently and what your dream sexual scenario would feel like. After you review those words, I want you to write down how you would know you have had great sex. What are you doing? What is your partner doing? What are you feeling? What is your partner feeling? This is how you move from sex as an achievement to sex as an experience.

These are the experiences that would fall under my definition of sex:

- An intimate discussion over dinner
- Snuggling in bed
- Kissing anywhere
- Helping each other during the day so we can relax and connect at night
- Showing compassion
- My partner touching my breasts
- My partner touching my vulva
- Me touching my own vulva
- Having an orgasm
- Giving a blow job

- Silly wrestling with or without clothes on
- Giving or receiving a compliment
- Talking about how we are going to please each other later

Congratulations! Your definition of sex is expanding! Way to go. When your definition of sex expands to include more of what you love, sex gets better. It becomes less goal-oriented and more experience-oriented.

The next step is understanding what makes you *want* your definition of sex. What makes you want to get naked and vulnerable? What keeps you from getting naked and vulnerable? No matter how you define sex, if you don't understand your arousal, pleasure and connection may continue to elude you.

Once you start expanding your definition of sex beyond penetration, orgasm, and performance, you begin to realize that something else needs an upgrade too: your understanding of arousal. Most of us were taught that arousal is a switch you either flip on or off, usually in response to something "sexy" happening.

But arousal is not that simple. It's not just a wetness or a hardness or a racing pulse. It's a slow build, a shifting landscape, a system that can be influenced by stress, trust, context, timing, and even the lighting in the damn room.

If you've only ever defined sex as a certain act, you've likely been taught to expect arousal to show up on cue and feel instant, urgent, and visible. But real arousal doesn't always work like that. Sometimes, it's subtle. Sometimes, it needs time. And sometimes, it needs a different door entirely, like scent, story, or slowness.

Expanding your definition of sex means making room for pleasure that's bespoke and personal. Expanding your understanding of arousal? That means honoring your body's unique pace, pathways, and preferences. You're not broken if arousal takes a while to show up. You're just human.

Let's talk about how it actually works:

"Hey, baby. What turns you on?"

Not super sure?

Good. This part is for you. This part of healing is where you fully understand your own arousal. It's important to hear the words *your own* because arousal is highly—and I mean *highly*—individual and contextual.

So you can throw those "*One* surefire way to turn them on" magazines in the dumpster and set them on fire. There is no "one surefire way" to turn anyone on. Arousal doesn't happen in a vacuum. Environment, stress, circumstances, and past experiences all play a part in when and how each of us gets aroused.

It is important to define the difference between desire and arousal. We throw these two words around like they are interchangeable.

They are not.

You can have the desire to have sex but have a hard time actually getting aroused for sex. The majority of people who show up in my practice have a desire to have sex. But actually getting aroused for sex is difficult.

It's wildly interesting to me that the body and brain sometimes do not play well together in arousal. Your body will respond to a sexual stimulus, like when your vagina gets wet when you see two people having sex on screen, even when your brain isn't particularly interested in seeking out sex with your partner in that moment.

This is called arousal non-concordance. Here is another way it may show up in your life: Maybe you aren't really feeling into having sex, but your partner begins to finger you. You say that you don't want to be touched right then. But your partner just grins and says, "Yes, you do. I mean, you're so wet!"

Has your body betrayed you? Are you really aroused and just don't know?

No. Your body is having a physical response to sexual touch. This doesn't mean you want to have sex. It's just like your mouth watering for food doesn't mean you are hungry.

Understanding arousal means acknowledging that your body is not a vending machine. You don't just push a button and get an orgasm. Your arousal system is more like a mood ring with a PhD in drama. It's sensitive to context, emotional tone, relationship dynamics, how your day went, what you ate, whether the sheets smell weird, and whether you feel safe enough to fully let go. This is especially true for people who were raised in environments that taught them their body was something to control, not listen to. If arousal feels inconsistent or confusing, it doesn't mean you're broken. It probably means you're operating under a set of expectations that were never built with *you* in mind.

Some people experience spontaneous desire—arousal that shows up like a sudden craving. But many others experience responsive desire—arousal that develops *after* stimulation begins. That stimulation doesn't have to be sexual at first. It might be emotional closeness, physical touch, a good laugh, or a moment of calm after a stressful day. Responsive desire says, "I wasn't in the mood, but I could be if the conditions are right." And that's not a lower-tier kind of desire. It's just *different*. It's also very common, especially for women, folks with trauma histories, and people in long-term relationships.

The biggest trap around arousal is the idea that it needs to be *felt* first, like some green light before you can begin. But sometimes, you notice arousal only once you've created space for it. You create the conditions and then *see if it wants to show up.* That might mean shifting out of go mode, moving your body, lighting a candle, kissing for more than three seconds, or just reminding yourself that you *don't* have to perform. You're allowed to simply explore. Curiosity is a more reliable arousal cue than pressure ever will be.

Activity: Map Your Arousal

Arousal isn't a formula—it's a fingerprint. This activity helps you explore your own turn-ons, turn-offs, and "maybe" zones so you can better understand how your desire works *for you.*

You don't need to know everything. This is about gathering data, not passing a test. Be honest. Be curious. Be kind to your past and playful with your present.

Part 1: What Helps You Feel Aroused?

These can be physical, emotional, relational, or environmental.

- What types of touch usually feel good to you?
- What time of day do you feel most open to sexual exploration?
- What kinds of communication make you feel safe or wanted?
- What sensory elements (lighting, music, scent, clothing, etc.) enhance your arousal?
- What role does emotional connection or mental stimulation play for you?
- Have you noticed any patterns—arousal increasing after laughter, rest, movement, or certain fantasies?

Part 2: What Disrupts or Delays Arousal?

Again, think holistically. Stressors can be physical *or* emotional.

- What shuts you down even if you were initially feeling good?
- What's your relationship to performance pressure or being "sexy"?
- Do you ever feel touched out or overstimulated?
- Are there beliefs, memories, or mental loops that tend to pop up during intimacy?

Part 3: The "Maybe" Zone

These are the gray areas—things that *might* work under the right circumstances.

- Is there a behavior or dynamic you're curious about but not fully sold on?
- Are there ways your arousal has changed over time?
- What could help you feel more open to exploring something new or different?

Optional Reflection

- What did this reveal about how your arousal *actually* works vs. how you think it "should"?
- What might you want to communicate with a partner about your arousal map?
- How can you create the conditions that allow arousal to show up, even when it doesn't start at the door?

Chapter 11: Rethinking Virginity

What if Mary (as in the Virgin Mary) wasn't actually a virgin?

Or, at the very least, what if I told you the term *virgin* didn't originally mean not having penetrative sex? Originally, the word *virgin* was used to describe a woman who was not married and had her own financial means.

And what if Mary's sexual behaviors were not the point?

The Latin root of *virgin* is *vireo*, which means "to be green, fresh or flourishing."[22] Flourishing! (Heart emoji) Another Latin root is from the word *virile*, meaning "strong."

A virgin: flourishing, strong.

A virgin was an unmarried woman—a woman who was free and liberated. A woman who was one with herself. When Hebrews used the word *virgin—almah* in original Aramaic—it defined a "young woman of childbearing age"[23] or one who had started her period and was now available for marriage.

For reference, *almah* is used nine times in the Hebrew Bible, and scholars agree that it does *not* refer to sexual experience.[24] Rebecca, Miriam, and the lover in Song of Solomon are just a few who are described as almah.

The first known use of the term *virgin* in English comes from AD 1200 and is found in a Middle English manuscript held in Cambridge. None of these uses describe sexual initiation.

Here is the real kicker: Mary, mother of Jesus, is not described as a *sexual* virgin until approximately AD 1300.[25]

Yes. The Virgin Mary is not described as a woman who hasn't had sex until 1,300 years after Jesus walked on this Earth. The first description of her as a sexual virgin came from an unknown author who was most likely a male, as they were the only ones who were getting published and cared about a woman's sexual experience. This description is in a book of Latin poetry called *Cursor Mundi,* which translates in English to *Runner of the World.* This was the first known author to use the word *virgin* to describe someone who was sexually inexperienced.

Bet they didn't mention these details in Sunday school. (Or Sabbath school if you grew up in the Seventh-Day Adventist tradition like I did.)

Christianity isn't the only religion or spiritual teaching that identifies its teacher, leader, or prophet as having a virgin mother. These other characters—mythical or historical—are also said to have had virgin mothers or to have been the result of divine conception: Buddha, Gilgamesh, Genghis Khan, Perseus, and Quetzalcoatl.[26] Ancient civilizations often claim a leader's miraculous entrance into the world as a sign of their influence and innate power.

You don't have to agree with all of these teachings or ways of believing to see the resemblance. All of these men have been described as sons of gods who came to Earth via a great woman. A strong mother. A flourishing virgin.

We typically hold Mary up as a standard of purity and chastity. The word *madonna* is defined as an "idealized, virtuous and beautiful woman." She is the highest in caliber for maternal care.

What changes for you when you also think of Mary as strong, flourishing, and independent—words that don't readily come to mind when we think of Jesus's mother? If we define *virgin* as strong, flourishing, and independent, how does that change your thoughts about what you were taught the Bible says about sex?

I'm often curious about the use of sexual vocabulary in the Bible. Most of us who grew up in a religious household do not question that Mary was a sexual virgin when she became pregnant with Jesus. But was she a virgin because she had never had penetrative sex? Or was she this more historically accurate definition of a virgin—simply young and menstruating? Or maybe she was considered a virgin because she was not yet married to Joseph. She was still *liberated*. She was strong and flourishing.

Since AD 1300, we have been focusing on her sexual status when we should be focusing on *her*. On how she was chosen to carry God's son because she was solid, steady, strong, self-aware, and mature. She knew what she wanted. She defined pleasure for herself.

Christians love Mary. They paint her, draw her, admire her, and worship her. She is a saint. Is it possible that in doing so, we also limit her? In the past 1,300 years, by labeling her a "virgin" in terms of her sexual experiences, we are devoted to keeping her "pure" and very little else.

Why do we do this?

Virgins in the Bible

Most scholars and Bible readers alike agree that women were considered second-class citizens in Biblical culture. The Bible is written through a male lens, and most of the characters follow suit. I'm curious to explore how the Bible describes the women who are mentioned. I want to know about the people who were like *me*.

Jesus had female disciples. In his book *Jesus Through Middle Eastern Eyes*, Kenneth Bailey[27] describes four texts that are significant in describing women as disciples. There is Tabitha (Dorcas), who is called mathetria (disciple). In Matthew's gospel, Jesus describes his brother, sisters, and mother as disciples—those who fear and do the will of the Father—using both female and male terms. In Luke 10:38, Jesus describes Mary as one who "sits at the Lord's feet and listened to his teaching."

Sitting at the feet of a rabbi like Jesus meant that one was a disciple. But the most interesting of all of these descriptions of female disciples is the description in Luke 8:1-3: "Soon afterward he went through the cities and villages, preaching and bringing the good news of the kingdom of God. And the twelve were with him, and also some women . . . *who provided for them out of their means.*"

What? Nobody ever told me this before! There were women in the disciple group who were paying the way for the disciples to move around, from city to city, out of *their own money*?

Who were these gutsy women?

These women were free (not married) and had their own financial means (probably skilled, mostly likely not young). *And* they were traveling with a bunch of dudes. They might have even been having sex with them. (Clutches pearls.) They definitely stepped out of the traditional roles defined for women of that era—or, at the very least, how we talk about those traditional roles today. They were blazing their own paths. They were supportive of a man who they understood would embrace and love them as women, second-class citizens.

They were badass. They were mature. They were confident. They were disciples of Christ. These women were liberated, free to follow, free to explore, and *free to find their own definition of pleasure.*

They were *virgins.*

Reflective Activity: Reclaiming the Word Virgin

Before You Begin

Take a breath. This is sacred, personal work. Whether you were taught that virginity defined your worth or were simply left confused by silence around it, this is your space to pause, question, and reclaim.

Part 1: What You Were Told

Take a moment to write down what you were taught about virginity—by parents, church, school, media, or culture.

- What *specific messages* did you receive about what it means to be a virgin?

- How was virginity connected to your value, morality, or future?
- Was there a moment when you felt changed or different based on sexual experience or lack of it?

Part 2: What You Believe Now

Let's dig into the shifts. Think about what you now know about the history, etymology, and cultural constructs of virginity as you consider the following:

- What parts of that old narrative still affect how you feel about yourself today?
- How would you like to *redefine* virginity, if at all?
- Could you imagine using words like *flourishing, strong,* and *independent* to describe your past or present sexual self? Why or why not?

Part 3: Create Your Own Definition

In your own words, write a new definition of *virgin*—or let go of the word altogether and create a statement about how *you* define sexual initiation, wholeness, or sacredness.

Examples to spark your thoughts:

- "A virgin is someone untouched by shame."
- "I don't use the word virgin anymore. I ask, 'Am I living aligned with my body and my desires?'"
- "A virgin is not a status. It's a season—a moment before awakening. And that moment can happen more than once."

Chapter 12: Rethinking Penetration

In the early twentieth century, a psychiatrist named Sigmund Freud (maybe you've heard of this walking red flag?) decided that after a female began menstruating, she should not be having orgasms through clitoral stimulation. He said that if a woman could not have a vaginal orgasm, she was considered childish and not sexually mature.[28]

Yes, you read that right. He said that if a woman could not have a vaginal orgasm, she was childish. He went even further and gave this phenomenon a name: *frigid*.

Gross.

And so we spent years and years and years thinking if we couldn't have a vaginal orgasm, we were cold, childish, infantile, and unsexual. We started to use the word *frigid* to describe low libido or a woman who isn't interested in sex.

Thanks to beautiful sexual health research institutions like the Center for Sexual Health Promotion at Indiana University, we now know that most women have their first orgasm—and most of their orgasms—through clitoral stimulation. So the "father of psychology" was telling us that we were frigid when we were actually amazingly wonderful women.

I don't want you to read that last paragraph without grasping that note about how most women have their orgasms through clitoral stimulation. That means touching, licking, and grinding—all on the outside of the body. This doesn't mean you don't experience good feelings with penetration. Of course you can! I'm just calling out how most women have most of their orgasms (and especially their first orgasms) through touch on the outside of the body. Most men, however, find more pleasure from penetrative activities.[29]

Why is this so important? Well, let me ask you how you define sex.

Go ahead. I'll wait.

Or maybe this question is easier: How do you define virginity? Or abstinence? Because if any of those definitions involve penetrative types of stimulation and if we know that most women have most of their pleasure from external stimulation, *we are defining sex through a penis lens.*

A lens that may not represent you . . . at all.

We were told that sex equals penetration. Out in the world, sex and penis-in-vagina penetration are synonymous. So, when you experience more pleasure with external clitoral stimulation than with vaginal penetration, you feel like you are not normal because *you* must not be doing it right.

It's exciting up here on my soapbox.

This message of penetration gets hammered into us (pun very much intended) with every scene and story about sex. Most romance novels, most porn, and most media will tell you that penetration is king.

Well, penetration may be king. But clitoral play is queen—and this is a *matriarchy*.

We must step away from the idea that sex can be defined and limited to one single, solitary act.

This is remarkably oppressive.

It's no wonder so many of us don't want to have "sex."

We are "frigid" because patriarchy's "sex" *isn't pleasant*.

Reflective Activity

Instead of defining sex as penis in vagina, write a paragraph that defines sex without using penetration at all. You may find yourself describing what you previously thought to be foreplay. But now you know it can be an active, wonderful, fulfilling sexual experience.

Chapter 13: Rethinking Porn

We give our power away to the thing we avoid the most.
— Unknown

When I was ten, I found a bunch of hidden porn magazines inside a hole in a pasture where I was riding my horse. Inside the hole was a stack of old magazines: *Hustler, Playboy,* and (drumroll please) *Guns n' Ammo.* The magazines were, in fact, not *current.* They were from 1974, and I found them in 1991. I distinctly remember one middle-spread photo: four women who were nude except for fur coats, socks, and platform heels. I remember thinking how ridiculous their outfits were.

Most of the women had unshaved or partially shaved vulvas. And all the women were linked together in some way—one maybe draping a leg over another one, who was sitting and holding the hand of a third woman. The fourth woman was squatting and about to lick the first woman's vulva.

My ten-year-old thought process was *This is so interesting! Look at these confident, naked women! This magazine is wild! I've never been that confident around other naked girls. I think those heels look uncomfortable. Wait, what is that lady doing?*

Then a rush of heat flowed into my cheeks. It was the first time I recall feeling ashamed of something visually sexual.

I threw the magazines back into the hole, covered it back up, and left. Quickly. I wasn't even sure why I felt bad, but I did. I felt horrible.

Later on, I figured out that the boys living close by that pasture were responsible for the stash. I looked a few weeks later, and all the magazines were gone. I don't recall ever telling anyone about them because I knew if I did, they would know I had seen the four women in fur coats.

Responsible ten-year-old Celeste was at an impasse. Something about the fact that these magazines were buried in a pasture made me think that they were somehow *not* good. But the other part of me *was very curious about the naked women in the fur coats.* Even as a responsible ten-year-old, I was grappling with a mix of curiosity and shame—feelings many of us associate with our first encounters with sexual content. But why does this curiosity so often lead to shame, especially when it comes to porn?

In a world that tells us an experience we are all naturally curious about is morally wrong, shame will always follow curiosity.

For clarification purposes, this is how I would describe pornography. Pornography is a form of media created with the primary intent to arouse. It typically depicts sexual acts, often exaggerated or idealized, and is designed to evoke a physical and emotional response in its audience. Like any form of entertainment, it reflects certain cultural narratives and preferences, often emphasizing fantasy over realism. While it can provide a space for exploring sexual expression and desire, its portrayal of intimacy is often shaped by market demands and creative liberties rather than an aim to educate or represent the complexities of real-life sexual relationships.

I often ask clients where they learned about sex. Often, the answer is porn.

"I found my dad's porn stash."

"I came across a video on YouTube."

"My friend showed me a website."

This is so common. And deflating. Because mainstream porn is not intended for education. *Everyone agrees with this.* People in the porn industry say this. Pastors say this. Parents say this. Porn stars say this. Porn-literate people say this. Porn-illiterate people say this. We all agree on this one thing.

Mainstream pornography is not supposed to be an education. It is created with the intent to entertain and arouse. Not to educate.

And yet, because of purity culture and a giant lack of comprehensive sex education, this is where a whole herd of us have our first encounter with the concept of sex. And it's where we continue to get our education about sex.

For example, let's pretend this following mainstream pornographic scene is your introduction to sex.

Thin, white woman lying by pool in a bikini. Perfectly round, gravity-defying D-cup boobs. We find out later that she is totally bald from the neck down.

Tall white man, chiseled abs, sharp jawline, bigger-than-average penis already erect in his trunks.

Seventy-five seconds later, he has his penis inside her vagina in a doggie-style position. She is huffing in ecstasy with a very audible orgasm at the same exact moment he climaxes. He has managed to bring her to orgasm without really ever touching her erogenous zones or her clitoris. The scene cuts to black ten seconds after they finish climaxing.

A simple scene? Maybe. But if this was your introduction to sex, this scene would make some impressions on your brain. Here are some fairly normalized messages that we get from pornography that, although specific to this scene, can be found in much explicit material:

- White, thin bodies are sexy.
- Big boobs are preferred.
- Sex is when the penis goes into a vagina. That is the way to feel pleasure, and those are the only two parts really needed.
- There doesn't need to be any time or conversation between meeting and penetration.
- The most important body parts are the penis and the vagina (not the clitoris).
- Big, erect penises are preferred.
- Orgasms are very loud and often happen at the same time.
- Consent is not verbal.
- No verbal communication is required before, during, or after sex.
- Shaved vulvas are preferred.

These messages are grossly exaggerated, incomplete, and, many times, false. Continued consumption (or comparing yourself to your partner's porn) *without* a normalized filter to counteract them leads to feelings of unworthiness and self-depreciation.

Please hear me say that this isn't your fault. Mainstream porn as education would absolutely not be an issue if we had excellent, shame-free, *comprehensive* sex ed.

Mainstream pornography is a problem because of *purity culture.*

Learning about sex by watching mainstream porn is like learning to drive by watching *Fast and Furious.* If you'd never seen a car, ridden in one, or taken driver's ed, you might think stoplights are optional, jumping bridges is routine, and crashes have no consequences.

Thankfully, driving isn't learned this way. From a young age, responsible driving is modeled for us. We watch adults stopping at lights, using blinkers, and navigating safely. Over time, we move from the back seat to the passenger seat, observing and asking questions, before ever taking the wheel ourselves.

The purpose of purity culture may have been somewhat rooted in good intentions. But, by devaluing sex and not giving us language, choice, education, and information, it inadvertently fueled the other side of everything it was trying to avoid. We are all still sexual beings, no matter how much some person or some institution tries to control the sexual narrative of our lives.

We are born seeking pleasure, and we die seeking pleasure in the same way we are born with a shade of skin, a color of eyes, and a first draft of a personality. The desire to be sensual, intimate, and connected is in the very DNA of who we are. We were born that way, and it is good. (A note about the asexual, or ace, community:

The desire to be intimate is always there for humans, even if it isn't sexual intimacy.)

So, we must explore that desire for pleasure to know it better. Just like we must explore what foods we like to eat, where we prefer to travel (or not travel), and what kind of music makes us dance the most ridiculously. Exploration is how we learn, and mainstream porn is the most accessible way to "learn" about sex. But in purity culture, even the thought of sexuality is denounced. So, here we are, sexual beings trying to understand our own bodies and feelings. Being told that we shouldn't have sexual thoughts while also desperately trying to understand our sexual bodies is utterly impossible. Impossible!

So what happened to us? The child, the teen, or the adult? It got us to the same place (sex) with fewer skills, more emotional pain, and more shame. We must be more dedicated to building a platform of healthy sexuality among our matriculating generations. (By simply reading this book, you are being more dedicated to building that platform. Well done!)

Beyond mainstream porn being bad sex education, folks tend to blast their other issues with porn out of proportion based on religious ideology, not science. More moral panic, less medical diagnosis. The vast majority of information people access about the negative effects of porn has been produced by religion-funded institutions (Christian, specifically) with an agenda of selling you accountability software and expensive "recovery" programs.

Interestingly, porn addiction is not a *thing*.

This is a topic of ongoing debate in the psychological, medical, and religious communities. Notably, the *Diagnostic and Statistical Manual of Mental Disorders, Fifth Edition* (DSM-5), published by the American Psychiatric Association, does *not* recognize pornography addiction as a diagnosable condition. This omission stems from a lack of consensus and sufficient empirical evidence to classify it alongside substance addictions.[30]

Research indicates that individuals with strong religious or moral beliefs may be more inclined to label their pornography use as an addiction, even when their consumption is comparable to that of nonreligious users who do not perceive it as problematic. This phenomenon suggests that the perception of addiction may be influenced more by personal beliefs than by the behavior itself.[31]

In their book *What Do We Know About the Effects of Pornography After Fifty Years of Academic Research?* McKee, Lisou, Byron, and Ingham indicate that porn is actually not the issue when looking at "porn addiction." The issue is the presence of sexual shame about the use.[32] Research on pornography often conflates causation with correlation and is moralistic rather than descriptive. Even scientists who find a problem* with excessive porn consumption state that moderate use is healthy.[33]

The problems that can be identified with neutral scientific study are most aligned with compulsive behavior. Compulsive sexual behavior disorder (CSBD) can apply to excessive porn use when it significantly disrupts a person's acts of daily living. Some examples might be using porn at work, missing obligations due to porn use, using porn to the point of constant procrastination, using porn as the only form of body regulation, and using porn to the point of creating arousal issues in partnered sexual behaviors. This is not the same as an addiction.

CSBD focuses on impulse control and not on addiction like substance-like dependency does. In these cases, research supports

---

* While excessive use can have negative effects, moderate use can be a natural and healthy part of life.

a behavioral approach that helps a person develop healthy coping skills to emotional triggers (overwhelm, loneliness, anger) without assuming they have addiction in a clinical sense. (If you are an elder millennial like me, you witnessed firsthand the correlation between the introduction of the internet—and specifically fiber internet, which serves video content without pause—and the increase in compulsive porn use.) At the end of the day, the issue isn't porn itself but rather the relationship a person has with it—a relationship often built on shame, miseducation, and purity culture.

But aren't the people in porn being manipulated? Abused and trafficked? Yes. This happens, and it's awful. Full stop. We need to be sure the porn we access is ethically produced. But did you know that the food production and domestic labor industries have far higher rates of human trafficking? The International Labour Organization reported in 2021 that 77 percent of trafficking victims were subjected to forced labor, whereas 23 percent were victims of commercial sexual exploitation.[34]

It's *far* easier to access and pay for ethically produced porn (bonus points if it is from a femme/queer/body-inclusive lens) than it is to guarantee that the orange you ate for breakfast was ethically produced without any manipulated, trafficked labor.

And what about the actors in explicit material? Aren't they just selling their bodies? I would say it's more like selling a performance. I don't know, like...an actor? And hopefully making good money doing it.

One of my favorite technology advances that straddles the line between sex work and porn is the introduction of webcamming. Camming (like OnlyFans) has created a way for sex workers to create personalized sexual experiences for clients without the risk of physical harm or STI transmission. They can also have access to clients across the globe and set their own boundaries, prices, and schedules. They can block abusive clients, enforce their own rules, and have autonomy over what they want to do without pressure from a manager or client. With the accessibility of platforms like this, sex workers gain much more agency, and the likelihood of coercion into sex work continues to drop.

All this to say: porn is complex and layered. My hope is that you walk away with just a little more clarity than you had before. In my work, most of the struggles I see around porn don't actually come from the porn itself—they come from comparison. People feel inadequate when they see what turns their partner on. They feel shame about what they're drawn to because they've only ever been taught to view explicit images through a rigid, religious lens—never through curiosity, context, or compassion.

The propaganda surrounding sex swings from one platitude to the next, and the pendulum swings the fastest through the middle, from black to white, pure to dirty, right to wrong. However, the middle is where we find freedom from binary thinking about porn. The middle is the wilderness, where nobody wants to admit to being but everyone actually lives.

Humanity is not binary.

So, let's talk about some healthy sides of ethically produced explicit material.

Yep. We are going there.

Just as there are benefits to an abstinence lifestyle as long as it isn't fueled by shame and is fully informed with comprehensive sex ed, there are also benefits to ethical explicit material…as long as it isn't filled with shame and is fully informed with comprehensive sex ed.

A bunch of readers of this very book have watched porn or watch porn regularly. Or your partners do. Or you watch porn together. However you feel about porn currently, I'd love to invite you to take an open approach to learning a bit more about it. I'm not asking you to embrace it. I'm just asking you to have a neutral curiosity about it.

My personal experience with porn is all over the place and has matured as I have matured. You already know my first experience, but I didn't have much after that until I started studying sexual behavior and getting educated through the American Association of Sexuality Educators, Counselors and Therapists. In taking courses to get my certification, I had to watch a lot of explicit material and really understand my own biases toward anything I was watching. In order to be a great sex educator, you have to be able to place your biases aside when speaking to anyone about any aspect of their sex life. This training helps us do just that. Nonjudgment doesn't exist. Only managed judgment.

So I've watched enough mainstream and ethically produced porn both for work and for pleasure to give me a good idea of what's available. The thing is, I've been working in the field of sex education for over a decade now. When I watch most porn, especially mainstream porn, it just feels, to me, kinda…goofy. (If I'm going to *enjoy* some spicy entertainment, you better believe it is going to have a fae penis, batwings and named Cassian.)

It's not that it doesn't produce an arousal response. It usually does because I'm a human being. But my years of exposure to normalized sex (talking to people about their real sex lives, researching and studying sexual behavior, and having sex myself) make porn feel more like entertainment and not intimidating. I've got a strong sense of what I like and don't like in sex. And I know what is feasible, accessible, pleasurable, and fun for me. I also know how to communicate these things to my partner and manage sexual conflict when it comes up. But that is *just me!* I've had *years* of sex ed to combat the noise about porn.

At the end of the day, I want you to have all the information you need to make a decision about porn that is right for you and your relationship. That means knowing your relationship and your partner's relationship with porn. That means negotiating with your partner over what feels within your sexual ethic. It might also mean exploring for more education and then making a decision about what fits and what doesn't fit for you and your partner. And finally, it means renegotiating it as you change and grow.

Finally, I'm not here to tell you what to do and not do when it comes to porn. I'm here to give you a gentle education and a viewpoint you may not have been exposed to. What you choose to do from there is up to you!

I'm forty-three, don't live under my parents' roof anymore, and have established my own sexual belief systems that determine my sexual behaviors. I want our collective children to experience agency and peace about their sexuality. I want them to experience something different. It's not that I don't want them to struggle. I just hope that their struggle is shame-free and filled with curious, autonomous exploration. I don't want it to be judged and influenced by oppressive institutions—the ones that fuel porn and the ones that fuel purity culture.

Activity: Reflecting on Explicit Material

What was your first exposure to explicit material? What education were you given about pornography, and how did it shape the way you feel about porn today? What current thoughts and feelings arise when you think about porn? What do you *want* to feel about explicit material?

Resource: Here is a list of ethically produced explicit material with a focus on femme perspectives. Even if you don't want to visit these sites, read through the list and notice what thoughts or feelings come up for you.

1. PinkLabel.tv

- **Focus:** Independent adult films with a strong emphasis on diversity and authentic representation
- **Highlights:** Showcases work from queer, feminist, and POC filmmakers, offering a wide range of genres and styles

2. Bellesa

- **Focus:** Female-friendly and couple-oriented content
- **Highlights:** Offers a variety of videos, articles, and erotic stories that prioritize female pleasure and consent

3. MakeLoveNotPorn

- **Focus:** Real-world sex videos submitted by everyday couples
- **Highlights:** Aims to normalize and celebrate authentic sexual experiences, moving away from performative stereotypes

4. Erika Lust Films

- **Focus:** High-quality, cinematic adult films with a feminist perspective
- **Highlights:** Known for storytelling, character development, and prioritizing female pleasure

5. Four Chambers

- **Focus:** Artful and experimental adult content
- **Highlights:** Blends eroticism with artistic expression, often exploring unconventional themes

6. CrashPadSeries

- **Focus:** Queer and gender-diverse content
- **Highlights:** Features authentic queer experiences with a focus on diversity and real pleasure

7. TrenchcoatX

- **Focus:** Curated, high-quality adult content
- **Highlights:** Cofounded by performer/director Kayden Kross and offering a range of genres with an emphasis on performer consent and creative control

8. Bright Desire

- **Focus:** Intelligent and intimate erotica
- **Highlights:** Combines storytelling with genuine chemistry between performers, aiming for a more realistic portrayal of sex

9. Feck

- **Focus:** Diverse and inclusive content
- **Highlights:** Emphasizes body positivity, consent, and authentic pleasure across a spectrum of sexual orientations and identities

10. XConfessions

- **Focus:** User-submitted fantasies turned into short films
- **Highlights:** Directed by Erika Lust and brings to life anonymous confessions with high production values and a focus on female pleasure

Note: When exploring these platforms, it's essential to ensure that the content *you* consume aligns with your personal values and comfort levels.

Chapter 14: Rethinking Masturbation

A common question I often receive is "Is it okay to masturbate?"

Physically and mentally, there are no health risks and many benefits of masturbation. Masturbation is a way to self-explore and get to know your own body. It's a beautiful conduit for you to experience pleasurable sensations.

I'm going to give you my thoughts on what the Bible says about masturbation because people ask me this *a lot*. You may not give a shit, and that's amazing! Just skip this section.

There is no indication in the Bible that masturbation is wrong. It became known as a "sin" from cultural contexts outside Scripture. The one biblical reference associated with the idea of masturbation is in Genesis 38, where Onan "spilled his seed on the ground" instead of impregnating his late brother's wife. We now understand that this is a reference to him pulling his penis out of the vagina before he ejaculated—or "pulling out." He was struck down by God because God wanted him to continue the lineage. But instead, he used the pull-out method to keep from getting his sister-in-law pregnant. So this one biblical reference isn't about masturbation either.

Masturbation is one way we explore what we like sensually. Think about how we explore food. We explore different foods to get to know what tastes good, what makes our bodies feel great, and, at times, what comforts us. We do not eat food for other people's pleasure. We eat food for our own pleasure and well-being. This is not a selfish act. Quite the opposite. This is an act of self-care and nourishment. We were born to eat! We have tongues full of taste buds whose *only* job is to taste and enjoy food.

Like with food, we are born to experience our sexuality. We are born sensual. (See the sensuality section in the last chapter.) From the time we arrive on the planet to the moment of death, we are sensual and sexual beings. And our bodies' sensations were created for us to use and explore through touch so we can live rich, full lives on this Earth—pleasurable lives. Just like the tongue has one job, you have an entire piece of anatomy (the clitoris) whose *only* job is to give you arousing, pleasurable sensations. Zero parts of the body are bad, from the tongue to the clitoris.

So yes, masturbation is one way you can experience your sensuality. It is a great way to get to know yourself in a safe environment and without the powerful influence of a partner. Because when it does come time for you to share your sensual self with another person, you *should* know what you like and what you don't like so you can *give or revoke informed consent to different types of touches and sexual acts.* It's difficult to give informed consent to a future sex partner when you don't actually know what you like or don't like. And it is not your future partner's responsibility to know your body better than you do. It is *your* responsibility to know your body.

Imagine if I asked you to make me my favorite meal but never told you what it was. When you come back with cheese enchiladas, I might feel completely heartbroken because my favorite meal is actually pesto tortellini.

Know what you like. Then, in the future, you can better communicate and help a partner know what you like.

So, if physically and mentally, masturbation has no health risks and many health benefits but you emotionally still feel a sense of shame or disgust around it, it may be up to you to explore why you have these feelings. They may be due to the messages you were given growing up. Or maybe a parent strictly told you not to touch yourself. Or somebody walked in on you masturbating and acted stunned. Even neglecting to tell a child about their own body and genitals sends an implicit message that they are somehow bad or shameful.

After exploring where you get these feelings or limited belief systems, you can decide for yourself if masturbation is right for you.

Activity: Reflections on Rethinking

Take a look at all the subjects in this section that your Healer is having you rethink.

List them here.

Circle the most uncomfortable ones.

What would change in your life if you began to think a bit differently about this topic? What would be easier? What are the risks? What would happen to your sex life?

As we close the chapter with the Healer, we leave wrapped in softness—with new truths held gently, old wounds given language, and a self more deserving than ever before.

But healing isn't the final destination. It's the threshold. We don't do all this inner work just to stay in the waiting room. The Explorer enters now—not to fix but to *experience*. She is your passport out of theory and into sensation. Where the Healer whispered, "You are worthy," the Explorer asks, "Now what do you *want*?"

This next phase invites you to get messy, curious, turned on, and totally free.

Part 4:
The Explorer

The Explorer is the part of you that has been waiting (sometimes whispering, sometimes pounding her fists) to *come alive again*. After the careful analysis, the burning down, and the gentle reeducation, she's the one who says, "Okay, but what if we try?" She isn't interested in theory or perfection. She wants *practice. Experience. Play.* She wants to taste, feel, move, touch, and speak. She is hungry—not in a desperate way, but in a way that signals *aliveness*. She is here to reclaim what purity culture tried to erase: your right to *wonder, wander, and want.*

For many of us, this is the scariest part. Not because trying new things is inherently dangerous but because we've been taught that *desire itself is dangerous.* That once you crack open the door to your own longing, everything will unravel. The Explorer dares to crack it anyway. Not recklessly but with *curiosity, consent, and consciousness.* She reminds you that exploration isn't the opposite of safety— it's the pathway to it. When you are allowed to explore your body, your needs, your pleasure, and your preferences without shame, you become someone who can trust herself.

This chapter is not about getting wild for the sake of it or checking boxes on some socially constructed to-do list. It's about *finding your edges and learning how to soften into them.* Maybe that means touching your body in a new way or using your voice during sex for the first time. Maybe it means fantasizing without guilt, wearing something you thought wasn't for you, or asking for what you really want. The Explorer is here to guide you not to a final destination but to the *next question.*

If the Analyst brought clarity, the Assassin cleared the wreckage, and the Healer created fertile ground, then the Explorer is the first bloom. Not polished. Not finished. But *thriving.* She invites you into the sacred art of experimentation—not to become someone else but to finally remember who you were before you were told to stay small.

Turn on your headlamp. It's time to explore.

Chapter 15: Explore Utilizing All Your Senses

Exploration doesn't begin with a wild new position or a trip to the sex shop. The Explorer isn't a thrill-seeker for the sake of chaos. She listens deeply to her body and makes bold choices *on purpose*. That means tuning into your senses.

Sensuality—your ability to feel, taste, hear, smell, and see with presence—is your compass. It's how you know what feels good, what sparks curiosity, and what quietly says, "Not yet." Without sensuality, novelty becomes performative. With it, every touch is a clue and every moment a chance to learn.

We use the word *sensuality* to describe sex a lot. When speaking to more conservative audiences, I sometimes switch out the word *sexuality* for *sensuality*. But it really isn't an accurate synonym.

Sensuality is simply the use of our senses. Have you ever watched a toddler sit in the grass? They are the most sensual beings. They are eating the grass, watching and listening to it blow in the wind, feeling it between their little fingers, and even smelling it. Nothing in their world could be more interesting than this grass at this moment. They aren't worried about what might happen to them later or feeling regret for something they said yesterday. They are simply experiencing the grass. And that is how they learn about grass. Done.

When did we lose this sense of exploration and curiosity? This way of utilizing our senses as a route to self-education? As we become adults, we want all of our education to come from books, online courses, and self-help gurus. But what about our bodies? Our senses are hungry students waiting to take in a waterfall of information at any moment.

In sex, our senses help us understand what we like. It is an education that is rich with creativity and change. Have you ever thought about what your favorite taste was during sex? What about your favorite thing to hear or look at? What gets your vulva aroused and your brain wanting more? All of this education is taught through your five senses.

Sensuality also brings us to the present moment. When you are lost in hypervigilance, tethering your mind to one or more of your senses brings you right back into the room and underneath the sheets. When you feel yourself drifting and thinking about that call you need to make in the morning, bring your focus back to one specific sense you are experiencing. The cool breeze of the fan on your butt. The warmth of your partner's skin. The sound of your head being scratched. The smell of your favorite Anthropologie candle. (The one you burn only during sex because you have taught your brain to smell the candle and get aroused, just like an erotic version of Pavlov's dogs.)

There is nothing better for leaving your thoughts, anxieties, and relived experiences outside your bedroom door than anchoring into one or more of your senses. It's a touchstone of presence. You cannot experience your senses in the past or future. You may be able to remember them or anticipate them, but you cannot *feel* them. Your senses are your gateway to living and finding peace and pleasure in this very moment.

Tuning into your senses isn't just a mindfulness exercise. It's preparation. It sets the stage for something deeper: *intentional sex*. When you're unlearning old scripts, healing from disconnection, or exploring something new, spontaneity can be overrated. Intention becomes your anchor. It says, "This moment matters." Whether you're lighting a candle that signals safety to your nervous system or deciding ahead of time to try a new touch, being intentional doesn't kill the mood—it *creates* it. It gives your body and brain time to collaborate, not just react. Pleasure extends when it's chosen on purpose.

Activity: Sensual Inventory: A Five-Sense Activation Ritual

This activity helps you slow down and reconnect with your body through your senses. You can do it clothed or naked, solo or with a partner, in silence or with music. Choose whatever feels safest and most inviting to your nervous system.

Set the Scene

Choose a comfortable space. Dim the lights if that helps you drop in. *Optional:* Light a candle, play soft music, or keep it quiet.

1. Sight

Look slowly around the space. What colors or textures catch your eye? Pick one thing to really *see*. Trace its edges with your eyes. Notice the shadows, shapes, and imperfections. You're not evaluating. You're just observing with curiosity.

Optional prompt: How do the visuals in this space affect your arousal, mood, or safety?

2. Touch

Run your fingers over different surfaces: your clothing, skin, furniture, or a soft blanket. Then place your hands on your body—your arm, belly, chest. Explore different types of touch: gentle, firm, stroking, squeezing.

Optional prompt: What kind of touch makes your body feel most alive? Most soothed?

3. Sound

Close your eyes. What do you hear right now? Let each sound enter your awareness without judging it. If you're playing music, let it wash over you. You can even hum or sigh. Use your voice as part of your sensory landscape.

Optional prompt: How does sound affect your turn-on, your focus, or your comfort?

4. Smell

Bring something close to your nose—a candle, lotion, essential oil, the fabric of your shirt, or your skin. Inhale slowly. What memories or feelings does it spark?

Optional prompt: Is there a scent you associate with safety or pleasure?

5. Taste

Take a sip of water or a small bite of something—chocolate, fruit, mint, etc. Let it sit on your tongue for a moment. Don't rush it. Let the flavors unfold. Swallow slowly.

Optional prompt: How does slowing down your eating or drinking feel in your body?

Chapter 16: Explore Intentional Sex (If You Don't Already)

As you move toward novelty, sensuality alone isn't enough. You also need intentionality—the conscious decision to engage with curiosity instead of being on autopilot. Too often, we chase "new" like it's the goal itself: new positions, new partners, new toys. But novelty without intention is like booking a flight with no idea where you're going or why. Intentionality doesn't kill spontaneity—it *gives it context*. It helps you explore in a way that feels aligned, grounded, and real. It's the difference between trying something to impress someone else and trying something because your body is whispering, "I think I'd like that."

I advise my clients to create intentional sex. I tell them to literally look at their calendar and make an appointment. Call it whatever they want. "Orchestra Practice" or "Making Origami Swans" or

"Fruit Canning." (This might also be a fun start for some sexual fantasy play.) The first thing most clients say is "Ah, no. I don't like scheduled sex. I want sex to be fun and spontaneous! Like when we first met!"

Oh, really? When you first met? Like that time you were both in grad school, were living in separate cities, and saw each other only on the weekends? Yeah! That was pretty good sex, huh? You spent every day during the week thinking about Friday night and how it was going to be amazing to see your lover . . . and enjoy all the fun, frisky things you would do to each other.

Or when you fell head over heels for each other at work . . . and you both couldn't *wait* to get off of your shifts and make a beeline to your apartment?

Or how you were best friends forever. But then, one day, you had that conversation and became a thing? And then you looked forward to every Thursday night because that was usually the night of Scrabble and more?

Everything was soooo spontaneous!

Or was it?

Actually, scheduled sex was happening even way back then. You just didn't recognize it as much. Maybe it wasn't labeled as "Couple's Scrapbooking" in your calendar, but it was pretty damn certain in your mind.

Yes, I'm sure there were times when sex was completely spontaneous and the act happened when you least expected it. ("Shit! I didn't shave!")

I've learned that when people say, "spontaneous," they mean they want sex to be "easy." Typically, sex felt easier when 1) everything was new and novel and 2) you had fewer responsibilities—the biggest killer of arousal. But we call this young, new, responsibility-free sex "spontaneous" when, in reality, we were thinking about it a *lot*.

You were thinking about the sex long before it occurred. You were thinking about what you might wear or not wear. About what you might do, see, or feel. You were thinking about the moves, the emotions, and the sensations.

This anticipation of sex is often, ironically, what makes sex feel "spontaneous." The thinking and daydreaming and planning of sex actually lead to easier initiation and arousal. When you have been in a relationship for a while, other things start to take up space in your brain. As a result, you start to think about and anticipate sex less.

Intentional sex in long-term relationships takes communication. Full stop. You have to look at your person in the eyeballs and say, "When would be a good time for arousal to show up for both of us this week/month/year/decade?"

Then you repeat this until you die dead.

I know, I know. I can hear all of you whining in my ear about this being "not romantic" and "killing the mood"!

I say this with love. Put your big girl panties on. This isn't a romance novel. This is your real, lived life, and you have to put energy into the things you want. Emily Nagoski does a great job of reminding us that our American society is obsessed with having the desire for sex. In reality, if we focused less on having the desire for sex and more on having an excellent, pleasurable, connective experience of sex, we would be having more and better sex.

Lay some communication down and start anticipating your arousal instead of waiting for your arousal to show up magically.

This is key. Intentional sex works because anticipation makes sex awesome. Anticipation about a scheduled event equals excitement.

On the flip side, anticipation about an unscheduled event sometimes equals anxiety and confusion. Here is another example: What is the difference in excitement level between the girl who is dreaming about getting married someday and the girl who has a ring on her finger and an event space booked? One is anxious, and the other one is anticipating.

Harness the phenomenal power of anticipation by communicating intention.

Now, what happens when you have communicated about a time to see if arousal will show up, but it doesn't show up? Maybe you ate too much pizza and feel gassy. Or your work drama keeps showing up in your brain and arousal doesn't show up in your undies. Or being intentional about sex actually just feels like pressure. First and foremost, communicate with your partner. Explain that arousal just isn't showing up for you. Then you both negotiate a sexual pivot.

Sexual pivoting means you have sex in a different way or at a different time. Sometimes, that means leaning into compersion (see Celeste's Suburban Dictionary for a full definition). Maybe your body isn't open to penetrative sex but is open to a cum shot (your partner coming on your skin). Or maybe oral sex is still on the table even if an erection is not. Other times, sexual pivoting means you move your intention for arousal to a different time.

Maybe in a couple hours or a couple days. No matter which way you pivot, the important thing is that physical connection and intimacy is still important and still on the table. Leave nothing nebulous.

Sensuality and intentionality together create the platform for true sexual novelty—the kind that feels expansive and not exhausting. Novelty isn't about being impressive or edgy. It's about staying open to discovering something *genuinely new* about your body, your desires, or your connection. This is what makes exploration sustainable. This is what makes it pleasurable.

And this is where the Explorer begins. Not with a dare but with a decision to be present, to be curious, and to let your senses lead the way.

Activity: Timing Check-In—When Is It a Good Time?

This activity helps partners explore when sex—or sexual curiosity—feels most possible and aligned. It's not about scheduling sex like a dentist appointment. It's about *learning your rhythms* and making space for pleasure that feels grounded, not pressured.

What You'll Need

A quiet space, fifteen to twenty minutes, and something to write with.

Step 1: Reflect Separately

Each partner answers these questions privately. Be honest. There's no right answer.

- What time of day does sex usually feel most inviting for me?

- What physical or emotional states help me feel open to arousal?
- What are the signs that I'm *not* in a good place for sex?
- What helps me *shift into* a sexual space when I'm not already there?
- When do I feel most connected to my partner (outside of sex)?
- What helps me transition out of go mode and into receive mode?

Step 2: Share and Discuss

Take turns sharing your reflections. Use these prompts to guide the conversation:

- "I notice I'm more open to connection when . . ."
- "Something that helps me feel available for sex is . . ."
- "A time that usually doesn't work for me is . . ."
- "I really appreciate it when you . . ."

Stay curious. The goal isn't to find a perfect formula—it's to understand each other better.

Step 3: Create a Shared Opening List

Together, consider a few situations or rituals that might help set the stage for sex (or the possibility of arousal). These are not commitments—they're invitations.

Examples:

- Saturday mornings after coffee
- After a shared shower
- When we light the candle that means "I'm open if you are"
- After we've had uninterrupted time to connect

Optional: Create a low-pressure code or signal for "I'm open to exploring tonight," like placing an object in a visible spot or sending a playful text. Initiation is often the most difficult part of sex, but creating intention around it eases pressure on both partners.

Chapter 17: Exploring Sex Toys

Listen. This is a moment about sex toys. If this isn't your *thang*, and you don't think it ever will be, you can just breeze through to the next section. No hard feelings. I understand that this isn't for everybody. But hear me out, y'all . . . You ask me about sex toys. All. The. Time. So, let's chat.

There are numerous ways to enhance the sense of touch. While on the quest to utilize your senses, I highly advise that you get creative. Do you love the feeling of silk lingerie on your skin? Does ice make you melt? What about the feeling of restraints? When you are utilizing all your senses (see above), you may want to explore the ways sex toys can give you different types of stimulation. Think of it like wearing cotton vs. nylon or stilettos vs. flip-flops. That's it. It just feels different.

Unfortunately, the biggest question I get about sex toys is "Will it replace my partner?"

Let me be clear: I don't care how many buttons, settings, vibration modes, spin cycles, beads, ribbed shafts, or Mariah Carey songs your sex toy plays. It will never replace the intimacy between two people. People with penises are especially worried that their partner's new King Dong 3000 will do exactly everything their own penis cannot. So, let me put this fear to rest.

While your partner's penis may not vibrate, they are the only one who can make your heart skip a beat when they walk into a crowded room. They are the only one who can kiss away your fears and make you laugh until you pee just a little bit. King Dong has nothing on your penis owner in the intimate connection department.

Let's all just calm down about this whole "replacement" theory. Sex toys are created to add some extra types of sensation and stimulation to your bedroom. That's it. (Now, if they come up with a dildo that tells me I'm smart, kisses me on the forehead, and vacuums my house, Imma have to throw out this paragraph. Somebody please get in touch with Roomba.)

Celeste's Sex Toy Dicktionary

Clitoral Toys

Clitoral toys are designed to stimulate the external part of the clitoris (a.k.a. the glans clitoris, located at the top of the vulva). But remember, most of the clitoris is actually internal, so even surface-level play around the labia goes deep and can stimulate the internal parts of the clitoris.

These toys aren't just for clits either. Try them on nipples, the perineum, or wherever it feels good. Just don't insert these into the anus, as anal toys should have a flanged base, and most clitoral toys do not. Some simulate licking or sucking, others have textured tips, and many are small enough to use during intercourse.

- **Bullets:** Small, powerful, and discreet. Great for beginners or anyone wanting a no-fuss vibe. Also known as "pocket rockets," they're easy to travel with and never go out of style.
- **Wearables:** Hands-free vibes that fit under underwear or sit in place. Many connect to an app or remote. So yes, your partner can tease you from across the room or the country. Dinner date, anyone?
- **Suction Toys:** Create a gentle vacuum effect that pulls blood to the clit, boosting sensitivity. Some include vibration for double the fun. Also great for nipples.
- **Air Pulse Toys:** These use puffs of air or a combo of air and suction. The air-puff-alone option can be a great choice for people with very sensitive clitorises.

Dildos and Dongs

Let's talk dildos. These are typically penis-shaped toys that have either a scrotum or a flared base (like a suction cup), which makes them safe for anal play or perfect for sliding into a harness. You'll find them in *all kinds* of shapes, sizes, and materials—from soft, squishy silicone to firm glass that's harness-compatible. (Yes, glass. Fancy.) Dildos and dongs typically don't vibrate.

People use dildos in harnesses for all sorts of reasons: some for prosthetic play—like when someone wants penetration and doesn't own a penis or can't get or keep an erection. Others use them for pegging, which is when a strap-on is used for anal play with a partner.

Some dildos look *very* much like a penis, others are just vaguely phallic, and some look like they came from an alien fantasy novel. Beam me up.

Oh—and a dong is basically just a dildo without the base or balls. It's still phallic—just a little less . . . anchored.

Masturbation Sleeves and Strokers

Masturbation sleeves—also known as strokers—are designed to add texture, sensation, and a little extra wow to penis play. They come in all kinds of shapes and functions, from simple sleeves to full-on robo-wizards of stimulation. Please, please, for the love of all things holy, always use a lubricant with masturbation sleeves and strokers. If a little penis pube gets caught up in there while jerking off, all the fun ends. Thank you and goodnight.

- **Basic Sleeves:** These are your go-to classics—about four to six inches long, open on both ends, with textured insides for added stimulation. Think of them as a soft, squishy upgrade to your hand.
- **Oral Sex Helpers:** These short sleeves can be used during oral sex to mimic deep-throating (without the jaw cramps). Bonus: They double as masturbation sleeves or can be used as a bumper during penetration to take off length and make sex more comfortable if you're the receiving partner.
- **Suction Sleeves:** These are housed in a case, are open on one end, and kinda have the shape of a large flashlight. When you insert the penis, air is pushed out and suction is created for a tighter, more intense stroke. Not to be confused with a flashlight in a blackout—unless you're looking for a very specific kind of illumination.
- **Auto-Stimulating Sleeves:** Let the toy do the work. These sleeves may vibrate, rotate, pulse, suck, or use massaging

beads to deliver next-level pleasure. It's like a personal assistant—but for the penis.

- **Stamina Training Sleeves:** Sleeves aren't just for fun—they're also great for building stamina and helping with premature ejaculation or erection challenges. Suction-based models and penis pumps are especially good at boosting blood flow and helping a penis stay harder, longer.

Multi-Function or Dual-Action Vibrators

Let's talk about toys that do more than one thing at once. These are often called dual-action vibrators—the *only* kind of multi-tasking I fully support.

Dual-action toys typically have a shaft for internal stimulation (which may vibrate, thrust, rotate, swirl, or even do that come-hither thing) plus an external piece that stimulates the clitoris or another erogenous zone at the same time. Basically? One toy, two jobs.

The most famous of the bunch is the Rabbit, made iconic by Charlotte in *Sex and the City*. After one memorable episode in 1998, rabbit sales exploded—and so did the conversation about women's pleasure.

They may look a little intimidating at first (mostly because of the handle), but they're not as bulky as they seem. Whether you're into vibration, suction, thrusting, or swirling—dual-action toys bring more than one kind of pleasure to the table. Practical is my kink.

Nipple Clamps

Most people think nipple clamps are just tiny torture devices. Slap 'em on, grit your teeth, and boom—instant pain kink. But actually? Clamps can do *a lot* more than just pinch. Some are adjustable and barely apply pressure at all. Some dangle cute little chains or sparkle with jewelry. Others buzz. (Yep, vibrating clamps exist.)

Here's the deal: The goal isn't always pain. Clamps squeeze the nipple, pushing blood out and making it go a little numb. Then— when you take them off—the blood rushes back in and, *voilà*, you've got hypersensitive nips. It's kind of like when your foot falls asleep . . . but make it sexy.

Whether you're into the look, the sensation, or the vibration, or if you're just curious, clamps are more versatile than they get credit for. They're not just for the hardcore—they're for the curious too.

Celeste's
Suburban Dictionary
of Sexual Behavior

I've studied sex academically *and* recreationally. Of course I have thoughts. Credentials and commentary are my two biggest assets (and here, size matters). This is certainly not an exhaustive list of sex moves. In fact, this is a pretty short list. However, these are the behaviors I get asked about most or the moves I really wish more people knew. Learn a little and take all my opinions *very lightly* . . . then explore and build your very own hot takes.

69: Overrated. On paper, 69 sounds like the dream: mutual pleasure, efficiency, and equality. But in practice? It's a logistical mess of managing angles, being distracted, and trying to give a performance while receiving one. It's the *hustle culture* of oral sex. Literally two people rushing to *do the most* at the same time, multitasking with their mouths, trying to be productive in both directions, and rarely slowing down long enough to fully *enjoy* it. Nobody's really present, everybody's a little overstimulated, and someone's probably overthinking their thigh placement. It's giving late-stage capitalism in position form. It promises mutual benefit but often leaves everyone a little underpaid in the pleasure department.

Aftercare: Aftercare is the emotional and physical care given after a sexual or kinky experience—especially those involving intense sensation or power dynamics. Just like a good workout or deep cry, sex and play can leave you feeling raw, floaty, vulnerable, or tender. Aftercare helps ground you. It might look like cuddling, talking, having snacks, checking in later, or just lying together in silence. It's not a weakness—it's an intentional way to support nervous system regulation and emotional connection.

In kink communities, aftercare is a core part of consent culture, not an optional extra. It says, "I see you. I care for you. And we're still connected." Because if you can spank someone, call them your filthy little whatever, and make them cry in a good way, you sure as hell better be able to hand them a juice box and ask how their inner child is doing. Honestly, aftercare might be my favorite part of sex. No cap.

Anal play: Yes, we are absolutely going to talk about anal play because people ask about this a lot, and there aren't great places to get good sex ed on this particular topic. I'm going to keep it straightforward. Anal play involves touching or entering an anus (with fingers, anal toys, tongue, penis, etc.) with the intent to provide pleasure.

Let's clear the air: Anal play can be pleasurable for anyone with a butt. The anus is packed with nerve endings and stretch receptors that respond to pressure, fullness, and movement. When stimulated gently and intentionally, those receptors can send delicious signals to the brain—especially when the person is already aroused. And for people with prostates, anal play can also stimulate the prostate (a.k.a. the P-spot), which can lead to intense, deep orgasms. But you don't need a prostate to enjoy anal. Plenty · of folks with vulvas experience anal pleasure thanks to the rich network of nerves and the shared internal wall between the anus and the vaginal canal. Translation: It's not about being "into butt stuff." It's about knowing how your body works.

The key to pain-free and safe anal play? Go slow, use lube like it's your (new) religion, and communicate more than you think you need to. Start externally with a light touch, massage, or lubed-up finger to warm up the area and see how the body responds. The anus doesn't self-lubricate, so silicone-based lube is essential. Breathing, relaxing, and staying present matter more here than in almost any other kind of sex because when the body is tense, the anal muscles clench right back. Let the receiver control pace and depth. And if anything hurts, stop. Pain is never the price of admission. And please—whatever you put in your butt should have a flared base or a handle. The anus is not a lost-and-found.

Finally, there shouldn't be any poop. Your poop remains farther up in the intestines until it is ready to make its grand exit. At that point, you will feel like you need to poop. If you feel like you need to poop, don't put anything up the butt until you have pooped. The end.

Compersion: This is the warm, satisfying joy you feel when someone you care about is experiencing pleasure, even if that pleasure doesn't directly involve or thrill you. In nonmonogamous circles, it often refers to the happiness you feel when your partner connects with someone else. But compersion isn't limited to polyamory. It shows up in all kinds of sex and relationships, often in quiet, everyday moments—like when your partner has a toe-curling orgasm and you're just lying there grinning like you won the lottery. Or when you watch them light up during something that's not necessarily your thing and you still feel lit up too.

In fact, when you do something that doesn't wildly turn you on *physically* but you feel joy *emotionally* because your partner loves it? That's compersion too. Take oral sex. Not everyone is obsessed with how genitals feel in their mouth. That's fair. But many people still *love* giving oral because of how it makes their partner squirm, melt, or moan. The pleasure comes from witnessing their pleasure. It's a beautiful, generous kind of arousal—not about tolerating but about *delighting in their delight*. Compersion says, "I don't need to be the one receiving to be deeply satisfied."

And no, this isn't about being self-sacrificing or performing pleasure to be a good partner. It's about finding *authentic* joy in shared experiences, even when your body's not the star of the show. You're allowed to say no. You're also allowed to say, "That's not my favorite, but I still love how much you love it."

Deep-throating: Deep-throating gets talked about like it's the big boss of blow jobs. Like it involves some final level of dedication and skill. But let's be real: It's not a blow job. It's a *stunt*. A performance. An impressive, high-level party trick that has very little to do with actual pleasure for the giver. It's about tolerating, not feeling. If someone tells you it's *the* move, ask them when they last enjoyed holding back a gag while trying to breathe through their nose. Exactly.

So why is it such a popular request? Because it looks extreme. It looks submissive. It's been mythologized in porn as the ultimate proof of enthusiasm or worthiness. As in, if you *really* like someone, you'll shove your airway aside to prove it. But you don't owe your throat to anyone. A blow job is about pleasure, not endurance. You are not a sword swallower at an erotic Renaissance fair.

You're a person with nerve endings, preferences, and a say in how things go.

If you love deep-throating? Hell yes. Do it with intention and a ton of flavored lube. But if you don't? You are not less giving, less sexy, or less good at oral sex. You're just someone who decided they'd rather keep their gag reflex intact. Gold star for that.

G-spot stimulation: Ah, the mysterious G-spot—a place so hyped that it's practically the Beyoncé of internal anatomy, except not everyone's into it and nobody can agree on where the hell it is. Let's clear this up: The G-spot isn't some magical internal button that unlocks orgasm like a cheat code. It's actually part of the internal structure of the clitoris. Specifically, it is the backside of the clitoris. (The clitor-ass?) It's not a separate pleasure center; it's the behind-the-scenes VIP area.

Now, let's talk about the branding crime. The *G* in G-spot stands for Dr. Ernst Gräfenberg, a man who, to the surprise of no one, *did not have one*. Like a snake naming shoes. Classic patriarchy. It's especially wild, considering people with vulvas have been exploring their own pleasure zones forever, but it took a guy in a white coat to name it for it to magically become important. And here's the kicker: Not everyone even likes G-spot stimulation. For some, it's amazing. For others, it feels like a polite "No, thank you" from their pelvic floor. So, let's stop pretending it's the Holy Grail of orgasms and start treating it like what it is: an optional side quest, not the main storyline.

Grinding: If you have a vulva, you probably aren't grinding enough. I could write an entire year's worth of inspirational quotes encouraging you to leave your leggings on and get up on that chest, thigh, FUPA, penis, washing machine, or pillow. If you asked your clitoris, she'd say she loves broad pressure. She doesn't want to be poked like an overworked Uber Eats driver smashing that doorbell. (Ding dong, nobody's home.) The clitoris is far larger than just the external glans. She has bulbs and legs underneath the labia that long to be pushed and palmed. Give her what she wants, and in return, she gets erect, signals your vaginal canal to secrete lubrication, and gets you hyped for anything else you might want to try. This is the only grind culture I support.

Kink: Kink refers to any sexual interest, practice, or dynamic that falls outside what's typically considered vanilla or conventional. That might include things like power exchange, sensation play, role-playing, bondage, or specific fantasies. Kink isn't about pain or dominance by default. It's about curiosity, creativity, and consensual exploration. At its core, kink is just another way people experience pleasure, connection, and expression. It doesn't require leather, whips, or a dungeon. (Though it can include those too!) It simply asks, "What if we played with this on purpose and with care?"

Kink also adapts and changes with time. At some point, French kissing was considered kink, but now it is normalized as vanilla or conventional. Kink can also be defined per couple or partnership or by an individual. What you may find kinky, I may find conventional. For the record, my kink is karma. ☺

Mutual masturbation: This sounds like it has to happen in perfect unison, like some kind of Olympic synchronized stroking event. But it really doesn't. It just means being sexual together while at least one of you is touching *yourself.* That could mean both of you doing your own thing side by side or taking turns. It could also be one person masturbating while the other watches, kisses, cheers them on, or whispers, "Holy sh*t, that's hot." It's not a backup plan for when you don't have time for sex. It *is* sex. It's intimate, revealing, and wildly underrated.

And yes, touching yourself *during* sex counts too. Mutual masturbation is a way to stay connected to your own pleasure while sharing it with someone else. It's not selfish—it's collaborative. It's like bringing your own dessert to a picnic and saying, "Hey, want a bite of this too?" Plus, it's a brilliant way to show your partner exactly what feels good without needing a whiteboard and a laser pointer. Your body knows things. Let it teach.

Mutual masturbation is often thought of as a "less than" type of behavior. But you are the expert in your own body, so being able to touch yourself to elicit the maximum amount of pleasure or show your partner what you like screams *agency*! If you haven't ever tried it, text your partner this right now: "Next time we have sex, I'd like to try touching myself."

RIP your phone.

Pegging: Pegging is when someone (usually a person with a vulva) uses a strap-on to penetrate their partner's butt. And if that makes you clutch your pearls, unclutch them. It's not about reversing gender roles or who's in charge. It's just butt stuff with accessories. Pegging can be playful, empowering, intimate, and wildly pleasurable. And no, it doesn't make anyone less masculine—it just makes them stimulated and well-loved.

Power exchange: Power exchange refers to a consensual agreement where one person gives up control (temporarily or ongoing), and another person takes it on. It can be playful, sensual, ritualistic, or deeply emotional. Think of it like role-playing with intention. One person may take on a dominant role and the other a submissive one, but everything is agreed on beforehand and can be stopped at any time. Power exchange isn't about one person being "better" or "stronger." In fact, the submissive often holds incredible power because the dynamic doesn't exist without their trust and consent. At its best, power exchange is built on mutual respect, deep communication, and care.

Activity: Erotic Sandbox

Use this erotic sandbox to understand and discuss which sexual activities you and your partner are comfortable with, are uncomfortable with, and would like to explore.

Directions

Create your erotic sandbox by drawing a large rectangle on a blank piece of paper.

Write down the sexual activities you are very comfortable with in the center of your rectangle. Write down sexual activities you have no interest in trying on the outside of your rectangle. Last, list sexual activities that you would like to explore (but that possibly make you uncomfortable) on the inside edge of your rectangle.

Use the lists below to help get you started! Enjoy having clear and fun discussions with your partner about what you both would like to learn more about and maybe even try.

Anal play

Arousal creams

Blindfolds

Blow job

Car sex

Eye gazing

Feather tickler

Fingering

Flavored lubricant

Flogger (soft, intense)

G-spot stimulation

Getting loud

Grinding (no penetration)

Hair pulling

Hand job

Lap dance

Movie make-out at
theater/home

Mutual masturbation

New positions

Nipple play

Oral sex on vulva

Prostate massage

Reading erotica together

Restraints (soft scarves,
straps, handcuffs)

Role-play

Sensual/genital massage

Sex in a new place/outside

Sex with music

Sex with the lights on

Shower/bath/pool sex

Spanking (hand, crop,
paddle)

Talking erotically or
"dirty"

Touching myself while
you watch

Touching new areas of
my body

Using a cock ring

Using a dildo

Using a lubricant

Using a vibrator

Watching ethical explicit
material together

Conclusion

Madonna Buder is an Ironman Triathlete.[35] The Ironman is a series of races. A 2.4-mile swim that's followed by a 112-mile bike race and ends with a 26.2-mile run—all in one day by the same athlete. Buder is in the US Triathlete Hall of Fame, and she gained her world record by crossing the finish line in 2012 in record time for her age bracket.

She was eighty-two years old.

Buder is also a nun at the Sisters for Christian Community. She began training for triathlon events when she was forty-eight as a way to bring relaxation and calmness to her body. She has competed in 390 triathlons,[36] 45 of which are the Ironman distance. Her world record is for being the oldest person to finish an Ironman.

But she didn't win her record without incredible challenges and disappointments. When she was seventy-eight, she missed the seventeen-hour cutoff time by seconds. When she was eighty, she had a wetsuit issue and couldn't complete the race. At eighty-one, she missed the bike cutoff by two minutes.

But at eighty-two—*at eighty-two*—she did it. She was the oldest and the *fastest* of the old.

They call her the Iron Nun.

She could have stopped racing, right? At eighty-two, one would have to consider retirement from such strenuous work, right?

Nope, not Buder. Not the Iron Nun.

At eighty-six, she earned the top spot in the next age group of the Olympic-length triathlon, and she keeps racing even at eighty-eight. When asked how her faith guides her training, she refers to her "five *D*'s."

"First, you have to Dream about whatever it is you want to do to fire up the second *D*, which is Desire. Then you need to acquire the Discipline and put forth the Dedication that will keep you Determined to do what you set out to do."[37]

Madonna Buder is gritty and resilient. She understands the importance of beginnings and the relativity of endings. She understands that life is lived in the water and on the road. Her moments of panic or joy or monotony while running or swimming or biking are the moments that matter.

It's not the pull-snap of finish line tape. Not the medals clinking together on the wall. It's not even the reporters and the cameras wanting to show her beauty and power to the world. Those are not what keep her coming back.

It is the brutal middle. It is the work. It is getting better and getting worse and getting smarter and starting over. That is what brings her empowerment and joy and freedom. That is what makes her heart sing and her sneakers tight. She chooses to enter back into the race. She chooses to feel the ache of tired muscles. She chooses to spend her time learning, assessing, and relearning her race. She chooses because she is independent. Emancipated. She is liberated. She is her own.

Like a virgin.

What now?

The biggest work of sexual agency is done for me, but the nuanced work still lives on. I've reached a place where sexual freedom comes in centimeters at a time instead of big leaps of realization and growth.

For example, I recently had to go through the deconstruction process to figure out how I felt about a certain sex act for my own sex life. I wasn't really sure how I felt about it, so I did the steps. Got into my backpack, addressed any shame, did some gentle re-education and had a vulnerable conversation with my partner. And ultimately, I decided I wasn't ready. And that is still growth because I developed a sense of *why* it wasn't going to happen, not just what wasn't going to happen. It was an *informed choice,* not a blind decision.

A centimeter.

My larger leaps are now in spaces of racial justice, reproductive justice, and body liberation. When you hear the word *intersection-*

ality, we are describing the work that looks the same in so many areas. When we know how to do the work in one area, we can start to do the work in other issues in life. What's in the backpack (internalized racism, internalized fatphobia, internalized misogyny)? What message is shame giving me? What does culture say? How have I been groomed? Where is my privilege in this space? How do I destroy the messages to find out what is true for me? What does my inner voice say?

What is an example of grit in your life? What did that feel like in the moment? What did it teach you about your future?

Your Feminine Power

One of the most surprising—and consistent—experiences I've discovered in working with women is this: we're walking around with far more power than we've been taught to recognize, much less celebrate. Not loud, bossy power. Not power *over* anyone. But intuitive, bone-deep power that shifts rooms, rewrites stories, and reclaims lives.

Before we dive into what that power looks like in your world, let's get clear on what we mean by *power* in the first place.

According to the *Oxford English Dictionary,* power is:[38]

> 1. The ability to do something or act in a particular way, especially as a faculty or quality.

> 2. The capacity or ability to direct or influence the behavior of others or the course of events.

We know that women make most of the financial decisions in the home as well as most of the millions of moment-by-moment decisions. In each of these moments, you are acting in a particular way with the capacity to direct or influence the behavior of others (soothing a child) or the course of events (whether there will be food on the table or not).

Power. We, as women, have been groomed to handle this particular kind of power. We have been told over and over that the power to parent, to cook and clean, to make household decisions, and to carry the cognitive load is the power that is "appropriate" for us because we have vulvas.

We also like to place men in a bucket when it comes to where they use their power too. For example, we groom men to handle the power of traditional work roles, which includes making the primary income and protecting the family. We think this is appropriate because they have penises.

Both ways of looking at us are incredibly limiting.

But just because these categories are limiting doesn't mean we're stuck in them forever. Power doesn't disappear—it transforms. And when we start to recognize the subtle, collective, and relational forms of power that women wield every day, we begin to understand something even bigger: our strength doesn't thrive in isolation. It multiplies in connection.

One thing we do know is: women are better together:

> New research in the *Harvard Business Review* finds that while both men and women benefit from having a network of well-connected peers across different groups, women who also have an inner circle of close female contacts are more likely to land executive positions with greater authority and higher pay, while there was no link found for the success of men in terms of the gender composition of their inner circles.[39]

Why is this? Why can men find success alone while women do better when supported by other women? Because women still face unconscious bias about advancement. And when there are other women around to help encourage, validate, and compare stories and strategies, we all rise in confidence and ability.

It's powerful to hear work stories from other women—especially when you're about to ask for a raise, apply for a better position, or do something terrifyingly bold. The power of other women doesn't come from perfection. It comes from their lived experiences, from the battles they've fought—whether they won or lost—and the lessons they've carried forward. What they've learned along the way becomes a map for the rest of us.

We weren't always this good at supporting one another. When only a few women held power, we were often forced into competition. We cannibalized each other for the one seat at the table. But things are changing. More women are showing up at every level— so the impulse to uplift instead of compete is growing. Slowly but surely, the table is getting longer.

I hope you've seen this shift in your own circle. Because the real magic? It happens when women support each other. I've been carried by women who've loved me through the most out-of-the-ordinary, earth-shattering moments of my life. They've made me laugh when I thought I couldn't, and their steady presence has become the bedrock of my confidence. I know—without a doubt—I wouldn't be who I am without them.

So I ask you: Who are those women in your life? Who's on your go-to contact list, your favorites tab, your emergency dial?

If you don't have at least a couple names that come to mind immediately, may I have this next dance? I want to be the head hype woman of your very own girl gang. When you try something new or are nervously tiptoeing out of your sexual comfort zone, I want you to envision all six feet of me hollerin' your name, telling you how proud I am of you, and screaming, "You got this" and "Get it, girl!" until my voice turns to squeaks and my eyes are bloodshot.

Because you are not alone. And you never have to be again.

Notes

[1] Eckhart Tolle, *The Power of Now* (New World Library, 2004).

[2] Brené Brown, *Braving the Wilderness: the Quest for True Belonging and the Courage to Stand Alone* (Random House, 2019).

[3] William H. Masters and Virginia E. Johnson, *Human Sexual Response* (Ishi Press International, 2010).

[4] Sarah E. Lantz, Jasleen Kaur, and Sagarika Ray, *Freud's Developmental Theory* (StatPearls Publishing, 2025).

[5] Abraham H. Maslow and Robert Frager, *Motivation and Personality* (Pearson Education, 1987).

[6] Stephen Diamond, reviewed by Kaja Perina, "Essential Secrets of Psychotherapy: The Inner Child," Psychology Today, June 7, 2008, https://www.psychologytoday.com/us/blog/evil-deeds/200806/essential-secrets-psychotherapy-the-inner-child.

[7] Brown, *Braving the Wilderness.*

[8] Manpreet K. Dhuffar and Mark D Griffiths, "Understanding the Role of Shame and Its Consequences in Female Hypersexual Behaviours: a Pilot Study," *Journal of behavioral addictions 3*, no. 4 (December 2014): 231–237, https://doi.org/10.1556/JBA.3.2014.4.4.

[9] "Shame," Merriam-Webster.com Dictionary, *Merriam-Webster,* accessed April 28, 2025, https://www.merriam-webster.com/dictionary/shame.

[10] Beverly Engel, *It Wasn't Your Fault: Freeing Yourself from the Shame of Childhood Abuse with the Power of Self-Compassion* (New Harbinger Publications, 2015).

[11] Greg Boyle, *Tattoos on the Heart: the Power of Boundless Compassion* (Manitoba Education and Advanced Learning, Alternate Formats Library, 2014).

[12] Brené Brown, "Shame Resilience Theory: A Grounded Theory Study on Women and Shame," *Families in Society: The Journal of Contemporary Social Services 87*, no. 1 (January 1, 2006): 43–52, https://doi.org/10.1606/1044-3894.3483.

[13] Arash Javanbakht and Linda Saab, "What Happens in the Brain When We Feel Fear," *Smithsonian magazine*, Smithsonian.com., October 27, 2017, https://www.smithsonianmag.com/science-nature/what-happens-brain-feel-fear-180966992/.

[14] Malcolm Gladwell, *Blink: the Power of Thinking without Thinking* (Back Bay Books, 2019).

[15] "Sexual Abuse," American Psychological Association, accessed April 15, 2020, https://www.apa.org/topics/sexual-abuse/.

[16] "Transforming Lives Through Healing Trauma," Somatic Experiencing International, traumahealing.org, accessed May 7, 2025, https://traumahealing.org.

[17] Sophia Cowley, "Why LEGALLY BLONDE Was An Impressive Feminist Film For 2001," Film Inquiry, November 8, 2018, https://www.filminquiry.com/legally-blonde-feminist-film-2001/.

[18] Naomi Wolf, *The Beauty Myth: How Images of Beauty Are Used Against Women* (Vintage Classic, 2015).

[19] Tamanna Nijjar, "The Forgotten Origins of the Body Positivity Movement," WWEDC, earingdisorderscoalition.ca, November 26, 2021, https://www.eatingdisorderscoalition.ca/blog/2021/11/26/the-forgotten-origins-of-the-body-positivity-movement.

[20] "Grandassa Models collection, 1963–1968," ArchiveGrid, reaserchworks. oclc.org, accessed October 4, 2018 https://researchworks.oclc.org/archivegrid/collection/data/858063084.

[21] Michaela Martin, "The Whitewashed, Diluted Reality of Modern Body Positivity: The Important Black History of the Body Positivity Movement," Student Life Student Wellness Center, The Ohio State University, u.osu.edu, February 18, 2021, https://u.osu.edu/studentwellnesscenter/2021/02/18/the-whitewashed-diluted-reality-of-modern-body-positivity-the-important-black-history-of-the-body-positivity-movement.

[22] "virgin," Online Etymology Dictionary: Origin, History and Meaning of English Words, *Online Etymology Dictionary,* accessed April 15, 2020, https://www.etymonline.com/virgin.

[23] Marvin Alan Sweeney, *Isaiah 1–39: With an Introduction to Prophetic Literature* (William B. Eerdmans, 2014).

[24] "Almah," Wikipedia.org, accessed April 2, 2020, https://en.wikipedia.org/wiki/Almah.

[25] "Cursor Mundi." Catholic Encyclopedia, newadvent.org, accessed April 28, 2020, http://www.newadvent.org/cathen/04574b.htm.

[26] Dr. Bart Ehrman, "Other Virgin Births in Antiquity" (live lecture), December 14, 2022, accessible via courses.bartehrman.com.

[27] Kenneth E. Bailey, *Jesus through Middle Eastern Eyes* (IVP Academic, 2008) [italics added by author].

[28] Katherine Angel, "The History of 'Female Sexual Dysfunction' as a Mental Disorder in the 20th Century," *Current Opinion in Psychiatry* 23, no. 6 (November 2010): 536–541, https://doi.org/10.1097/YCO.0b013e32833db7a1.

[29] Emily Nagoski, *Come as You Are: the Surprising New Science That Will Transform Your Sex Life* (Scribe, 2015).

[30] Erin Martinez-Gilliard, *Sex, Social Justice, and Intimacy in Mental Health Practice: Incorporating Sexual Health in Approaches to Wellness* (Taylor & Francis, 2023).

[31] American Psychological Association, "Religious, Moral Beliefs May Exacerbate Concerns About Porn Addiction," APA Newsroom, apa.org, February 6, 2020, https://www.apa.org/news/press/releases/2020/02/religious-moral-porn-addiction.

[32] Alan McKee, Katerina Litsou, Paul Byron, and Roger Ingham, *What Do We Know About the Effects of Pornography After Fifty Years of Academic Research?* (Routledge, 2022).

[33] Kathryn Fotinos, Andrea Sansone, Alexandria Greifenberger, Martin A. Katzman, Tommaso B. Jannini, Yacov Reisman, Erika Limoncin, and Emmanuele A. Jannini, "Pornography and sexual function in the post-pandemic period: a narrative review from psychological, psychiatric, and sexological perspectives," *International Journal of Impotence Research 36*, no. 7 (2024): 706–714, https://doi.org/10.1038/s41443-023-00812-3.

[34] "Human Trafficking 101," U.S. Department of Transportation, transportation.gov, updated April 14, 2025, https://www.transportation.gov/stop-human-trafficking/human-trafficking-101.

[35] Madonna Buder and Karin Evans, *The Grace to Race: the Wisdom and Inspiration of the 80-Year-Old World Champion Triathlete Known as the Iron Nun* (Simon & Schuster, 2010).

[36] NTD Newsroom, "88-Year-Old 'Iron Nun' Is a Triathlete Champion," NTD.com, March 18, 2019, https://www.ntd.com/88-year-old-iron-nun-is-a-triathlete-champion_301762.html.

[37] "88-Year-Old 'Iron Nun' Is a Triathlete Champion."

[38] "power," *The Oxford English Dictionary* (Oxford University Press, 1992).

[39] Shelley Zalis, "Power Of The Pack: Women Who Support Women Are More Successful," *Forbes*, March 7, 2019, https://www.forbes.com/sites/shelleyzalis/2019/03/06/power-of-the-pack-women-who-support-women-are-more-successful/#5ea650ac1771.

Additional Resources

Books

Advancing Sexual Health For The Christian Client: Data and Dogma by Beverly Keller Rachel Dale

Bonk: the Curious Coupling of Science and Sex by Mary Roach

Expanding the Practice of Sex Therapy: an Integrative Model for Exploring Desire and Intimacy by Gina Ogden

Good Christian Sex: Why Chastity Isnt the Only Option--and Other Things the Bible Says about Sex by Bromleigh McCleneghan

Intuitive Eating: a Revolutionary Program That Works by Evelyn Tribole and Elyse Resch

Jesus Feminist: an Invitation to Revisit the Bibles View of Women: Exploring the Radical Notion That Women Are People, Too by Sarah Bessey

Sex God: Exploring the Endless Connections between Sexuality and Spirituality by Rob Bell

Sex, God, and the Conservative Church: Erasing Shame from Sexual Intimacy by Tina Schermer Sellers

Sexual Intelligence: What We Really Want from Sex—and How to Get It by Marty Klein

The Erotic Mind: Unlocking the Inner Sources of Sexual Passion and Fulfillment by Jack Morin

The Purity Myth: How America's Obsession with Virginity Is Hurting Young Women by Jessica Valenti

The Vagina Bible: The Vulva and the Vagina—Separating the Myth from the Medicine by Jen Gunter M.D.

Untamed by Glennon Doyle

Other Sources

"Changing the Face of Medicine | BarbaraRoss-Lee." U.S. National Library of Medicine. National Institutes of Health, https://cfmedicine.nlm.nih.gov/physicians/biography_279.html

"You Are Good—A Meditation," Hillary L McBride, https://hillarylmcbride.com/you-are-good-a-meditation/

Abbey Rose Maloney, "The Influence of the Kardashian-Jenners on Fourth Wave Feminism Through Digital Media Platforms," *Elon Journal of Undergraduate Research in Communications 8,* no. 2 (2017). https://www.elon.edu/u/academics/communications/journal/wp-content/uploads/sites/153/2017/12/05_Feminist_Maloney.pdf.

Xavier Lalanne-Tauzia and Katya Lopatko, "Scholars Say If You Hate the Kardashians, You Probably Hate Yourself," Vice, https://www.vice.com/en_us/article/d35a9x/scholars-say-if-you-hate-the-kardashians-you-probably-hate-yourself

Acknowledgments

First—and yes, foremost—I'm giving myself credit. For believing I could write (and maybe even sell?) a weird-ass sex book that's somehow both unsexy and irreverent. Believing in yourself isn't arrogance—it's what the boys have been doing all along. So here's your reminder to believe in your wildest weirdo dreams too. And for the love of all things unholy, give yourself some damn credit.

Next, my husband Nate, the finest beard and the steadiest soul. Thank you for loving me through every fierce doubt and wildest idea. I'm the luckiest.

Alisha, my BFF—you are in every word, I wouldn't be here without you. erin, you created the original archetypes and fueled this book with borrowed grit and BDE. Monika, thank you for making this manuscript more/less crayon depending on the page. Deborah, the most positive, progressive MIL I could ever dream of. Muy inteligente! Clare, my muse. Wayne-o, total cheerleader. Terria, constant. And Jen, your support means ever more than you know. Thank you for putting me on the map.

To Mikey, Carly, Soups! and the *Big Idea to Bestseller* crew—
thank you for making this dream real. Rachelle, you believed
in me through it all. Marcelle, Lesley, Brittan, Dana, Lilly,
Amanda, Shelby, Kimber, Angela, Lisa, both Saras, Margaret,
Ashley, Shalah, Miriam, Aunt Pam, Josie and Oliva. To the boys:
Joe, Matt, Dave, Chris, and MJ – you are chosen brothers I will
always cherish. To all the Rogue Women, the Irreverent Launch
Team and every single client —you each held a corner of this
story.

Devon, I promised to live more adventurously after you died. I
hope this book counts. (At least it would've made you laugh.)

Mom, thank you for making me read *Hiroshima*, watch *Roots*,
and see Maya speak. You knew from the beginning I'd be a slow-
burn advocate, and you led the way. Every brave thing I've ever
done is because of you.

Dad—thanks for laughing so hard we almost got kicked out of
the hospital waiting room when I showed you the title of this
book. It made the whole thing worth it. When God made you,
filled with gentleness and love, They called you good. Every kind
thing I've ever done is because of you. (Sorry about all the fuckin'
cussin'.)

Made in the USA
Coppell, TX
12 June 2025

50660664R00125